GOLF
CHING

GOLF
CHING

Golf Guidance and Wisdom from the *I Ching*

TERRENCE MACCLURE

**Andrews McMeel
Publishing**

Kansas City

Library of Congress Cataloging-in-Publication Data

MacClure, Terrence.
    Golf ching : golf guidance and wisdom from the I ching / by Terrence MacClure.
        p. cm.
    ISBN 0-8362-2716-6
    1. Golf—Psychological aspects. 2. I ching. I. Title.
GV979.P75M32 1997
796.352'01'9—dc21   97-561
                                                                CIP

The author can be reached at terrence@holonet.net

See page 137 for photo credits and permissions.

ATTENTION: SCHOOLS AND BUSINESSES

Andrews and McMeel books are available at quantity discounts with bulk purchase for educational, business, or sales promotional use. For information, please write to: Special Sales Department, Andrews McMeel Publishing, 4520 Main Street, Kansas City, Missouri 64111.

Abide by the spirit of the game:
Play the ball as it lies.
Don't touch the ball with anything
but a club until it's holed out.

—*old Scottish golf rule*

Accept your circumstances.
There is nothing to blame.

—*the* Golf Ching

For my wife Cindy and my son Miles.

CONTENTS

ACKNOWLEDGMENTS

I would like to thank *I Ching* translators Richard Willhelm, Cary F. Baynes, and John Blofeld; authors John Beebe, *Integrity in Depth,* and Robert Grudin, *The Grace of Great Things;* the archives at Corbis-Bettman, the United States Golf Association, and St. Andrews University.

INTRODUCTION

I play golf.

And I'm fairly serious about it. A few years back I started practicing seriously, every day. One day, driving home after a particularly tiring, demoralizing stint at the practice range, I asked myself why I was doing this. Why did I obsess over this game? And why should I put up with such an unenjoyable time practicing? I was now tired and a little depressed. Perhaps I had become too serious. My life was not on the line, but one would think it was. I needed, badly, to know why I was playing and practicing. Because I was a hairbreadth away from giving the game up. Again.

I grew up on a golf course. I lived on the fifth fairway of a private course known simply as "The Village," about a five iron away from the green. I played competitively. I practiced long hours, and I taught myself. I studied golf instruction books till late at night, often falling asleep with a club in my hand. I assembled hundreds of photos of professional swings to study further and to emulate. In short, I talked and lived golf.

When it came time for me to leave home, and The Village golf course, I found my way (or lost my way, depending on how you look at it) to another golf course to live near and work. I would prepare myself to turn professional. Friends I had competed with had turned professional, and some had started showing up on the tour. So working at a golf course and making golf a career was a natural step for me.

On the first day of work at my new course, I was told the automatic ball picker had broken and all the range balls needed to be picked up by hand. There were hundreds and hundreds of balls sitting out there on the range. I was given a small hand picker. I still remember the blur coming over me as I stood in front of a sea of golf balls. I laid the picker down, walked to my car, removed my golf spikes, put on my shoes, and drove off. I never returned to work. I never quite understood that moment fully other than I knew that picking up those balls would make an ugly imprint. But the damage was suddenly done. Golf, in that moment, became utterly meaningless. Twenty years would pass before I played another round.

Now, as I was driving home from practice, these events crossed my mind again. The feelings I had now were very similar to the ones I had had twenty years ago standing before a white sea of golf balls: *This game is so stupid because it has no meaning whatsoever.* But now, twenty years later, I was better prepared to fill this empty situation. When I returned home I went straight to the bookshelf, found the *I Ching* consultation book, and asked, "Why? why do I do it?"

The *I Ching*

For the uninitiated, the *I Ching* is the most ancient of the Chinese classics whose purpose is to dispense wisdom to anyone who sincerely desires it. *I Ching* literally means "change book." Several figures had a hand in forming the book's basic ideas. The first was legendary emperor Fu Hsi, who lived in the third millenium B.C. Most scholars agree that it was King Wen, a popular Chinese leader in the twelfth century B.C., who greatly expanded the ideas of the *I Ching*, presented them in a logical order, and added comments. This was supposed to have happened while Wen was imprisoned for a year by a jealous emperor. King Wen's son, the duke of Chou, then overthrew the emperor and founded a dynasty. During this period, the son expanded on his father's thoughts.

Confucius, China's most celebrated philosopher, added his commentaries to the *I Ching* in the fifth century B.C., stressing it as a book for ethical and correct conduct.

The *I Ching* dispenses wisdom in a couple of ways. First, it helps clarify your situation so completely that the way is open for proper action. Some say the clarity of one's situation is made so clear that the future becomes obvious. Thus, it sometimes seems able to *predict* the future.

Second, it gives advice on correct action and conduct, making it a book of ethics or ways, means, and conduct.

Not until 1949, when the famed psychologist Carl Jung wrote an introduction to what was to become the most popular English translation of the *I Ching*, by Cary Baynes, would the *I Ching* take root in the West. That introduction is now one of the most memorable modern essays in understanding the *I Ching* and most likely contributed to its popularity.

The Philosophy

The *I Ching* observes that everything is governed by one law: *all things change*. The ancient Chinese believed that the *I Ching* contained the means to managing change by breaking it down into sixty-four manageable changes. By relating one's personal affairs to one of these changes and following the specific guidance, one was better able to manage life. In the *I Ching*, these sixty-four changes are also known as "hexagrams" (the *Golf Ching* calls them "lessons"), because each one is pictured as six lines, broken and unbroken. Each hexagram has a slightly different combination of broken and unbroken lines that gives it a particular character.

A Common Introduction

I was introduced to the *I Ching* several years ago by a Jungian analyst who casually opened the book one day to help answer a question I asked. I don't remember the question, just the sensation of the answer being correct, its incredible accuracy, and, above all, its usefulness. This seems to be a common and almost universal introduction to the *I Ching*: someone has a ripe problem and a friend who happens to have the *I Ching* on a bookshelf. I was immediately smitten, and for the next few years I went every week to this analyst just for a tutorial in the *I Ching*. Ever since, I have used it successfully for wisdom and guidance for myself and others.

A Lesson for Golf

When I got home I asked the *I Ching*, "Why am I doing this? What could you possibly have to say about my golf game?"

To find my answer, I took three old coins, laid them down six times in keeping with the tradition of finding the correct hexagram/lesson in the *I Ching*, and located the answer:

It read: Lesson 4 *Youthful Folly. Immaturity. Inexperience. Still Learning.* Meaning, my game is full of youthful folly, immaturity, and inexperience. And I'm *still learning.* This was sobering. After I read further, the *I Ching* also seemed to be answering the question "Why should I play?" And it was to this angle I began to take heed.

I should continue to play this game because I love to learn (I also love to teach). This is what gives my life meaning. And it was possible, most probable, that this was why I started playing in the first place and a good reason to keep on playing. *Why not learn something new?* Curiously, that thought had never occurred to me. I was continuing to practice by myself as I did as a youth. Maybe this was *youthful folly.* And since I had never taken a proper teacher (unlike my friends who turned professional), I may have stayed relatively immature and inexperienced.

Since the *I Ching* is helpful in naming what is changing in your life and gives suggestions on how to manage it, it named the change I was going through in my golf game. It suggested that I best manage this change by accepting the idea that I was still learning the game (who isn't?) and that I'd better start acting on it. Here was the buried meaning from my youth. It was also the meaning now.

Because of this lesson, I acted on a long-buried impulse: I wished I had a great teacher to teach me the game all over again. A few months later, I found a great golf professional. Although he lives far away from me, one of his students is close by to take lessons from.

The *I Ching* was not finished. It cited six suggestions or stages in this changing time of learning:

1. Offer encouragement and support to the inexperienced.

2. Be kind to inexperienced players.

3. Be careful of imitating and absorbing someone else's swing.

4. Be careful of performance fantasies, as they can sometimes be humiliating.

5. When seeking instruction, be unassuming so you can be taught.

6. When correcting others or yourself, do not be hard, punishing, or intrusive; it doesn't help.

It's a meaningful and moral code.

> *I was playing a round the other day at a beautiful links-style course with my weekly playing partner, Herb. We were paired with two guys who had a little trouble getting off the tee. Then a little more trouble. Then some more trouble. All the way down the fairway. Herb was groaning as he stood on the green watching one of these guys blast buckets of sand, but no ball, out of a links-style deep bunker. Eight strokes later, I walked up to the bunker and said, "Can I make a suggestion?" The guy replied, "Sure." "Open your club face very wide. Aim your body left of the pin. Hit two inches behind the ball. Let the sand carry the ball out." With those words, and one shot, he was out of the trap. And miraculously close to the pin. "Thanks." "Sure."*

"Offer encouragement and support to the inexperienced." "Be kind to inexperienced players."

The lesson of teaching and learning (lesson number 4) is, in my case, concerned with more than just mechanics and playing better. It is concerned with meaning and proper conduct. It is concerned with managing how to be and act during this meaningful and changing time.

Over the next year, I consulted the *I Ching* several more times on matters pertaining to golf. But the mystery of what the game meant to me had been solved and I was satisfied. What was left was the pile of notes I had compiled about golf, based on consulting the *I Ching*. So I kept on going, transposing and reinterpreting the remaining sections of the *I Ching* to fit the game of golf.

THE GOAL

The goal of the *Golf Ching* is to *suggest* a way to understand and proceed with your game, particularly in times of anxiety, meaninglessness, or dissatisfaction. The suggestions will be satisfying if you have the willingness and sincerity to seek and follow some advice. Traditionally, an oracle is consulted when you're at a crossroads and need some guidance on how to proceed.

Here is an example. A women's golf club champion called me asking for advice. She was a golfer at a club I used to belong to. She told me she had lost her title of club champion the year before because of an injury. (She had dropped a frozen chicken on her foot.) Even though her injury had passed, she was still playing poorly—so poorly that she was no longer enjoying the game. The next morning she was to play in a partners tournament and was concerned that her play would bring the team down. She wanted a magic swing diagnosis and prescription. I asked her about her ball flight, her short game, etc. We talked about some swing mechanics.

"No, no, no," she said. "None of this is going to work. It's the whole thing. I wish I could just start all over. But that would take years."

She was fed up. The coincidence of her calling me at the same time that I was finishing this manuscript was too great a temptation to dismiss. Since she had remarked, "It's the whole thing," I suggested to her that it might help her to have a deeper understanding of where her whole game was at. After I gave her a short explanation of the book and principles, she followed the method of finding a *Golf Ching* lesson. She received two lessons.

The first lesson read: *The type of joy you're experiencing from your game is such an allure that you can be swept aside.*

This is what was happening now. The allure of trying to play well was so great that it had swept her aside. The joy she was desiring depended on playing well and winning her championship back. She was unable to focus on anything else. I explained to her that the way she was attempting to fix her game was luring her far away from herself and the real situation. She agreed that the *Golf Ching* had indeed named the situation correctly, and we moved on to the second lesson.

The essence of the second lesson read: *Realize that other players enjoy your company and your game. They enjoy your form of confidence in yourself and in them. In some way, shape, or form, your sincerity helps other players.*

After I read this lesson to her, she offered me this story: She had run into a club member at the grocery store. This member told her, "I wish I had your game. You're such a good player."

"Oh no, no, no. There aren't any good players around here."

"Oh, don't say that. You're better than I'll ever be. For a long time I've been wanting to tell you that it's because of you I'm still playing."

She related this to me because it was the message of the second lesson. The lesson focused her attention on this small social event and gave her permission to receive it differently. This recollection was now a significant coincidence and an important reference.

She went on. "Last night, I got a call from the other two players in my group. They asked me if they should bow out because they weren't playing well. They didn't want to spoil the fun. I told them that that was ridiculous. I'm playing lousy. Get out there and play. "

I said, "It seems as if the *Golf Ching* is telling you that people really enjoy playing with you. They're depending on your sincerity and confidence. This information is important to receive and focus on."

I took it for granted that these two lessons were restorative for this player. Her attention had shifted from the alluring mechanical fix of the game to another part of the game that had been trying to speak to her. A month later I talked to her and the issue of the lesson came up. She said, "Oh, yeah, that. Well, I knew that. People love playing with me." The lessons were so obvious that they were effortless. Often, this effortlessness is the experience of a deeper understanding of one's game.

THE METHOD
OF CONSULTATION

There are two basic ways to consult the *Golf Ching* and find your lesson.

1. The simplest way is to open the book anywhere and find an interesting lesson to which you can relate. Read it through, and try applying it for a while.

2. The other way is more complex but well worth learning. This method will produce the exact lesson and lines for you to read based on asking the *Golf Ching* one basic question. It is very much like going to a golf pro and asking him to observe your swing so he can give you advice about your game.

The Question

What do I need to know about my game now?

The *Golf Ching* provides guidance by answering this core question about your golf game. Make a slight variation in the question if you wish, but, essentially, this is the question the *Golf Ching* is best suited to answer.

Finding Your Specific Lesson

1. Take three coins (pennies work well), shake them, and drop them on a table.

2. Tally the value by counting heads as two and tails as three. The possible values are 6, 7, 8, and 9. Example: three heads equals six, two tails and one head equals eight.

3. If the tally is even (6 or 8), draw a broken line (__ __). If the tally is odd (7 or 9), draw an unbroken line (_____). Put the number

value (6, 7, 8, or 9) next to the line. A line with a value of 6 or 9 is called a changing line. Make a notation next to any changing lines.

4. Let the coins drop again. Tally the value. Place this second line above the first line you drew (not below). Keep going in this way until you have stacked six lines. The six stacked lines are called a hexagram (in the *Golf Ching* "lesson" is used instead of hexagram).

This is what a lesson might look like (this example is Lesson 4):

$$
\begin{array}{ll}
\text{—— ——} & 9 \\
\text{—— ——} & 8 \\
\text{—— ——} & 8 \\
\text{—— ——} & 8 \\
\text{————} & 7 \\
\text{—— ——} & 8 \\
\end{array}
$$

5. All lessons have one of sixty-four possible numbers. To find your number, look on the chart in chapter 6. Look for the bottom three lines of the lesson (referred to as "lower") in the left-hand column of the chart and the top three lines (referred to as "upper") along the top of the chart. Where the upper and the lower intersect on the chart, you'll find your lesson number.

Try finding the lesson indicated by the example above. Look for where the lower and the upper intersect on the chart, and you should find Lesson 4.

6. Next, go to the chart in the back of the book and find your lesson number. First, read the text, but *not* the individual lines. Then find the changing lines (the lines with the numerical value 6 or 9, next to which you have placed a notation). Read only these lines. (They are called changing lines because they have tension— enough tension that they verge on changing into their opposites.)

Look again at our example. Find Lesson 4 in the section of lessons and read the text. In our lesson there is one changing line, Line 6, which has a value of 9. Read Line 6 of the lesson and disregard the other lines.

7. If there are changing lines in your lesson, it means you have yet another lesson to find and read. Changing lines change into their opposites. The significance of this is that your situation is changing into the second lesson.

Change any of the changing lines into their opposites.

In the above example, the top line with the value of 9 is a changing line. After changing this line into its opposite, it looks like this:

Line 6	____ ____	changed from unbroken to broken
Line 5	____ ____	8
Line 4	____ ____	8
Line 3	____ ____	8
Line 2	_____	7
Line 1	____ ____	8

Now look up this lesson's number on the chart. You'll find it is Lesson 7. Now read about Lesson 7, leaving the lines alone.

8. The purpose of the second lesson is to show what your situation is changing into. You may notice some elements of the second lesson happening now.

9. If you have a lesson with no changing lines, there is no second lesson. Some people like to read all the lines in this case, just to help familiarize themselves better with the lesson. But no particular line applies at this time.

10. If you have two lessons because of a changing line or lines, the first lesson can be seen as a way of understanding golf now (or what you need to abide by now) and the second hexagram as suggesting where your game may be headed.

A PRACTICE

You do not have to be in a crisis, desperate, or anxious to use the *Golf Ching* (although despairing times are common in golf). You can use the oracle as a practice to become more familiar with the sixty-four aspects of life.

1. For eighteen holes of play, consult the *Golf Ching*. Ask "What would be helpful for me to know about my game today?" See if you can place your attention on the matter the *Golf Ching* suggests.

   Use this as a way to direct yourself for the day's round or practice. This can be done for every round to gain direction for the day and to become familiar with the different situations and conditions.

2. For a lesson that is appropriate for a longer period of time, find a lesson for yourself and stay with it for a while. For example, some players have stayed with the same lesson for a year. You may find the lesson becomes easier to relate to and deepens over time.

THE LESSONS

1. POWER

distance, force, strength

Be aware of how much strength and power you use in each situation.
Move the ball with the right amount of force every time.

Golf power ebbs and flows. What we can do is use what power we
have appropriately for each shot. This is a good attitude—physically,
mentally, and emotionally—for any kind of shot in any type of
situation.

This image is of Ben Hogan driving. Hogan, a small player who
wielded great power, is symbolic of always using what power you
have to your advantage. He was one of the longest and most accurate
drivers of his time. Never had the ball been struck with more accurate

force than it was by Hogan. Notice the perfectly balanced finish position and the sense that nothing has been wasted.

stages of power

LINE 1 · The majority of your strength is still hidden and therefore not yours to direct. Take it easy so you don't tire yourself.

LINE 2 · You can feel your power, but don't show off with unthinking shots.

LINE 3 · Look for moments of golf power you can direct and guide.

LINE 4 · Sometimes the power of your swing can seem unfamiliar. Yet it is exhilarating.

LINE 5 · Enjoy the flight of the ball that at times seems to come out of nowhere.

LINE 6 · Watch out for complete abandon of the use of force.

2. THE RECEPTIVE

accepting, yielding, responsive,
power to sustain and nourish, less is more

Accept things as they are. This exudes warmth, growth, and nourishment.

This lesson is about softness and receptivity. You can find this principle embedded in players who are very accepting of their ball lies, circumstances, and shots. These players are warm and responsive. This lesson advises you to be grateful for playing partners who are nourishing, supportive, and complimentary. It is time to withdraw from being aggressive or competitive. It may be time to play a reflective game.

This image is of Walter Hagen sitting and enjoying the flight of a partner's ball. A receptive pose. Hagen had charm, warmth, and acceptance. His character was what made the touring professionals acceptable and finally got them through the front door of elite clubhouses. He once remarked to someone about a terrible lie, "There is my ball, and there I must play it." Great power in acceptance and receptivity.

stages of receptivity

LINE 1 · Don't resist the way your game is. Especially the way it begins.

LINE 2 · Don't struggle. Less is more.

LINE 3 · If your game goes well, don't look for recognition. Just hold to *your* experience of your game without outside acknowledgment.

LINE 4 · You and your game are tied up. At this time you don't have easy access to changing it. And to do so would be dangerous.

LINE 5 · Love this game. It's for the greater good of the game.

LINE 6 · There is a lot of struggling going on. Too much.

3. DIFFICULTY

difficulty at the beginning, growth pains, struggle

Golf is difficult at the beginning: when you are first learning, when you are trying something new, or simply when you are starting a round or a season. See the difficulty as something trying to grow.

This lesson focuses on the struggle with something new. Possibly with new habits coming or old habits leaving. Whatever part of your game is struggling because of new growth, this lesson shows you that in spite of the difficulty, or because of it, you will traverse it. This is a time when something about your game is or needs to be under some kind of repair. And this repair will come about.

This image is of new ground. New shoots are arriving. You can't hit on it or walk on it. You must take a drop from it. Slowly it grows and becomes part of the course again. This part of your game ought not to be relied on greatly. Let it repair, improve, and grow. When it strengthens, integrate it back into your game.

stages of difficulty

LINE 1 · It's difficult to get better at something new immediately.

LINE 2 · Your golf game can seem as if it's falling apart. Getting better has its own time frame.

LINE 3 · You can feel lost learning new habits. Rely on feedback and guidance.

LINE 4 · You have been waiting for more shots to click. And they can with someone's help.

LINE 5 · It is clear what to do, but new habits are not strong enough. Do what you've been practicing in small ways.

LINE 6 · Sometimes the game is just so difficult it seems like blood and tears. But this passes.

4. TEACHING AND LEARNING

acquiring experience, youthful
folly and inexperience, immaturity

Golf is for learning and teaching. Without that, it is youthful folly.
Seek guidance. Give guidance.

This is about areas of your game being inexperienced and about finding an experienced teacher. This allows you to acquire experience, coordination, and maturity.

This is also about teaching. If you are an experienced teacher, know when someone is receptive to what you have to offer. If you perceive habits that are a barrier to what you have to impart, then it is best to stop and wait until the player is ready.

There is a caution: Be careful of asking too many questions of teachers, otherwise you can get confused and doubtful as to how to proceed.

This image is of Bobby Jones instructing. This great player is taking time out to give a lesson, give some pointers, if only for a minute. A great player, he also took time to pass on his understanding of the golf game in a book.

stages of teaching and learning

LINE 1 · Offer encouragement and support to the inexperienced.

LINE 2 · Be kind to inexperienced players.

LINE 3 · Be careful of imitating and absorbing someone else's swing.

LINE 4 · Be careful of performance fantasies, as they can sometimes be humiliating.

LINE 5 · When seeking instruction, be unassuming so you can be taught.

LINE 6 · When correcting others or yourself, do not be hard, punishing, or intrusive; it doesn't help.

5. WAITING

calculated inaction, exhibiting the power to wait

Waiting is inevitable. Use this time wisely. Know what kind of waiting is called for. And always find a way to nourish yourself while waiting.

A large part of the game is waiting. You might as well get good at it. The most obvious time is waiting on the tee or fairway for the group in front of you to move ahead. You don't hit into them because it is dangerous. There are dangers on the course in which different types of waiting are called for.

This image is of Ben Hogan waiting. Hogan was the most exacting player in the game, taking every nuance and every aspect into account. He was also known as "the wee ice mon" and "the hawk" for his cold ability to concentrate. Here he is concentrating on nourishing himself while he is waiting.

stages of waiting

LINE 1 · There is a type of waiting that is once removed. Act as if everything is normal and fine, no matter what.

LINE 2 · While waiting to hit a dangerous shot, be careful about listening to self-talk that is conflicting. Stay calm.

LINE 3 · Sometimes we have to wait so long we're bogged down. We could lose our momentum. Change the perspective by taking a small walk.

LINE 4 · In circumstances such as an awful lie, where nothing you can do will help, there is nothing you can do but accept it and wait to let whatever happens happen.

LINE 5 · There is a waiting that is literally fun. There is drinking, merriment, laughter, and general nourishment of everyone. Don't forget your strategy, though.

LINE 6 · Sometimes, even by waiting, you will not know what to do. Occasionally, advice arrives in strange ways. Intuition. Outside interference. This happens.

6. CONFLICT

conflict, argument, dispute

*When you experience conflict, take a
step back to reclaim a bigger perspective.*

Conflict in golf is inevitable. Conflict can take the form of thinking you
are right and your playing partner or teacher is wrong. You may find a
shot strategy to be best when another is tempting. Very tempting. In any
case of conflict, one part of you goes one way and the other part goes another, which lessens your ability to make a clear-headed shot decision.
You may also be in conflict as to what is the best technique or method.

This image shows at least two members of a rules committee looking
at a ball lie. The question is probably whether the ball can be moved

somewhere else. The man above the two men kneeling is taking a further look, and this is significant in this lesson of conflict. He represents the ability to take a step back and remove oneself, however slightly, from the closeness of the conflict.

stages of conflict

LINE 1 · When any conflict begins, in yourself or with another player or teacher, drop it right at the beginning.

LINE 2 · When a conflict is clearly stronger than you, step back.

LINE 3 · Be careful of getting inflated during a conflict—again this means with yourself and others—as your game will be left behind and will suffer.

LINE 4 · There is a type of conflict that you could win—but you're wrong—so it's best to step back again, realize this, and change yourself.

LINE 5 · This conflict needs a rule book, another member of your group, or any other outside influence with a cool, clear head.

LINE 6 · The worst kind of conflict is when you carry something through to the bitter end, win, and irritate yourself or everyone else.

7. THE ARMY

group, need for organization, coordination

Find the best part of you to lead the charge and make decisions.

This is called "the army" because it means the ability to organize your resources. Golf can become a battle when danger (or even winning) threatens. And when it does it's best to know who's in charge. It is that part of you that makes the best, strongest, and most confident decisions so that the rest of you follows along.

This image shows Palmer surrounded by his crowd. They faithfully follow and are known as "Arnie's Army." Arnie is a strong leader who has enormous reserves inside himself. We are like this at this time, calling upon our own reserves to lead the army inside ourselves.

stages of organizing

LINE 1 ʼ Be sure you have good reason if you are to be charged up. If not, keep cool.

LINE 2 ʼ Be in touch with the welfare of your entire game in the midst of charging through any shots.

LINE 3 ʼ An aspect of charging is failure. It sometimes happens. It's because you've led your passion in an inferior way.

LINE 4 ʼ This aspect of leading your own passionate resources requires stopping and not using them.

LINE 5 ʼ There are shots when you see what you want to fight for and it's time to do that. Use emotional maturity.

LINE 6 ʼ When your game has ended, remember to rely on the exceptional ability part of you. Rely on that part. It takes time to stop the lesser parts.

8. HOLDING TOGETHER

union, unity, cooperation, coordination

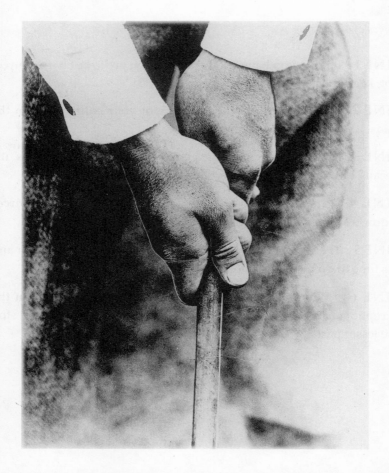

Attend to gathering your hands together in cooperation. Then, everything cooperates. This is no less than gathering and holding yourself together.

Coordination depends upon the union of forces. In golf, your hands unite the forces at work. Although placing your hands on the club may seem mechanical, we are often reminded how important the grip is. Here, it is a gathering together of much more than mechanics: Your honesty, sincerity, confidence, gratitude, and persistence all come together. This union reverberates throughout your game and character.

This image is of Bobby Jones's hands on his club. Notice how they are gathered "together." They unite easily and simply. The rest of his game, character, and quality was held together by this simple act.

stages of unity

LINE 1 · There is confidence in how you unite and coordinate your game.

LINE 2 · The sense of unity in your game comes from you alone, *then* move it outward.

LINE 3 · What is gathering in your game doesn't seem to be helpful. It's off the mark.

LINE 4 · In this kind of gathering, something new in your game is integrated.

LINE 5 · Now, a few elements in your game are not cooperating. They're cut off from your intention.

LINE 6 · Here, there is a lack of willingness in your game. There is little coordination because of this lack of will and leadership.

9. THE TAMING POWER OF THE SMALL

soft and gentle, the restraining
power of the gentle, the lesser nourisher

Less is more. Look at what is seemingly small and
gentle about your game. Have smaller expectations.

To be effective now, "small" has the greater influence. Such as smaller expectations. There is less likelihood of being disappointed, and you can value what you're good at to the fullest extent. This is how "less" can be put to good use. Consider this the "small path." It's not a bad way to go for now.

This image is of "wee" Bobby Cruickshank, one of the smallest competing professionals. Here, he looks as if he's circling the ball with the determination of a lion tamer. His was certainly a small taming power, hence "the taming power of the small."

stages of less is more

LINE 1 · Even though you may have momentum in your game by following a course of action, slow it down. You may be meeting with opposition. So, think small.

LINE 2 · Stick with the basics, even though they seem small. This returns you to where you may have started with the game.

LINE 3 · When the wheels fall off your game, do not blame anyone. Do not blame yourself. Wheels will *always* be falling off.

LINE 4 · Know that the basics of the game will always restore your consistency and confidence. This is important because your confidence has an effect on others.

LINE 5 · Notice that your consistency and confidence breed friendships. These qualities help bring people together. Find something small and basic to harbor these important qualities.

LINE 6 · Be careful about how you ride out the confidence in your game. Right when your confidence is restored, the wheels have a tendency to want to come off again.

10. CONDUCT

moving cautiously, stepping carefully, treading

Move carefully. Be cautious in what you say and do. Be gracious. Be generous.

This lesson is about how you conduct yourself during a potentially treacherous situation. It's just like treading water: You don't make any erratic movements. Just smooth movements. Be careful how you tread, for example, on your playing partners. There is a need for good and appropriate conduct. You can change irritability to cheerfulness in yourself and in others with your conduct.

The image here is of Francis Ouimet congratulating winner Johnny Goodman of Omaha after Ouimet had lost this semifinal match of the U.S. Amateur Golf Championship. Both are exhibiting simple, gracious conduct. Ouimet could be upset inside and therefore treading on dangerous ground: his own potential eruption over the loss. But it is not noticeable. It is not there. Notice the policeman behind the players. Good, gracious, simple conduct is the law here.

stages of conduct

LINE 1 ꞏ Be simple in your conduct as you go your accustomed way to play your game.

LINE 2 ꞏ Move along with solitude. There are times this is necessary in order to practice and accomplish in your game what you want. Anybody looking to improve his game is, at one time or another, reclusive.

LINE 3 ꞏ Do not lean on your weaknesses as an excuse for not seeing or doing something about your game. You are not less capable. At the same time, don't be dauntless with your game.

LINE 4 ꞏ Now your game is in a hazardous situation. Because of your caution, you can lead yourself through it.

LINE 5 ꞏ You may think your game is strong or you are right about an aspect of the game. This leads to unavoidable trouble. Use some delicacy. Be particular to cause a minimum of upset if you must tread on the beliefs or thoughts of others.

LINE 6 ꞏ This is a time to look back on how well you've conducted yourself during times that have been trying. Good conduct is an accomplishment.

11. CONTENTMENT

peace, harmony, prosperity, greatness

*Whatever your game, wherever you play, contentment
exists when everything you perceive fits and has its place.*

Peacefulness and contentment exist because opposites exist together:
small and weak, strong and vigorous. The strength of this perception
and lesson is the ability to keep everything in perspective. This can particularly apply to relationships with playing partners and with yourself. It is a time when being small does not work. Being big does. This
is seeing how one thing leads to the next and is connected.

This image is of the sixteenth at St. Andrews, Scotland. Notice how
everything moves so beautifully. Note the distinctions of valleys and
hills and how one moves into the other and back again; the shadows

and light, which do the thing; the meandering, yet firm fence; the clear boundary of skyline meeting the fairway. None of these can exist without its complement. Everything is distinct, yet connected. It is an image of contentment and peacefulness.

stages of peace and contentment

LINE 1 · Notice what is connected. For example, in divots, from grass to roots.

LINE 2 · Do not disregard your companions. In the service of including what is small or distant, be determined to pay attention to acquaintances and players without turning this into a club.

LINE 3 · Don't label anything good or bad. Particularly any eclipse you may have had. Things move and change. Your game. Your abilities.

LINE 4 · Notice any moving back and forth: of indecision, between fellow players, between your resources and others'.

LINE 5 · Something that has been missing from a player returns and develops quickly and vigorously.

LINE 6 · This is not a time for force. Hold your reserves. Don't force your theories of golf on yourself or anyone else. Just maintain yourself.

12. STANDSTILL

frustration, stagnation, obstruction

This frustration is best managed by knowing it is not caused by you but by the inevitable. You can make progress gradually even when frustrated.

When elements of your game are disconnected, there is frustration, a standstill, a sense of stagnation. It is the opposite of the previous lesson of contentment because now things do not come together. They move apart. Such as the hole and the ball. It is a type of frustration that is not caused by you. It is caused by the times. You simply go through it by withdrawing a little and using less force. Generally, by sticking with the frustration you will make gradual progress.

This image is of Lee Trevino in a moment of a standstill. There is not much you can do to influence the standstill. You can only make useful suggestions to yourself in order to make gradual progress. This allows you to move through this inevitable time.

stages of frustration

LINE 1 ᐧ At this time of frustration, your game is not *that* bad. You can persist in what you think is the right way for you.

LINE 2 ᐧ Now, it's best to have some patience. Your game is trying your patience. It's almost distressful.

LINE 3 ᐧ Now, your game is shaming you. Shame comes from not living up to an ideal. Do not let this ridiculous shame-producing ideal interfere with playing fully now.

LINE 4 ᐧ Your game now is the result of the way a teacher has informed you or of staying with some highly regarded principles of the game. Even if you're frustrated, you've done well to try what has been suggested.

LINE 5 ᐧ Stagnation in the game always ends. It ends here as well. But you must remember that your game could collapse again.

LINE 6 ᐧ The frustration of the game suddenly ends. This is such a relief you're almost joyous.

13. FRIENDS

like-minded people, human associations

Share what you have about the game of golf.

The lesson here concerns beneficial relationships in the game of golf: with playing partners, teachers, associations, theories, and ideas. The suggestion is that your game can benefit enormously because of your associations.

This image is of Arnold Palmer and Jack Nicklaus. They are like-minded, and they are friends. Their successes were helped by their friendship. Palmer was on the rise and took center stage as Nicklaus was just emerging. Nicklaus then began to rise and took center stage.

stages of friendship and association

LINE 1 ' A union with a person, association, teacher, or idea is just beginning and can help your game.

LINE 2 ' A golf friendship with someone who is *too* much alike does not really help the golfer or the game of golf. It's more of a mutual admiration. It broadens nothing. And it could condemn other golf groups and teachings. This kind of association can lead to humiliation.

LINE 3 ' Sometimes no benefit shows in your golf game through new ideas and associations. This could be because of mistrust. It happens in friendships. Mistrust leads to a long wait.

LINE 4 ' A barrier exists. Between you and teacher, playing partners, associations, or golf theories. But now you know the barrier is there. You're beginning to accept the different things you see.

LINE 5 ' Friendships such as these can make you weep or laugh. Competing, playing, or practicing the difficulties you have with these "friends" leads to a stronger understanding of the game.

LINE 6 ' The attachment to a cherished golf idea, playing partner, or teacher isn't there anymore. But all of them are still part of your golf life. Warm feelings and closeness with them can come and go. What remains is your understanding of them.

14. POSSESSION IN GREAT MEASURE

great possession, many blessings

When you succeed in finding the great part of your game, remember to be
modest and generous toward other players. This is the Great Possession.

Great Possession is concerned with the successful golf character:
strength, clarity, and richness in resources. But, also, the ability to see
and emphasize the greater good even in the face of miserable things
happening.

In this image we see the "Great Bobby Jones" and his great possessions:
his major victory trophies for one of the greatest amateur records of all
time. What Bobby Jones had in great measure was his character of
strength and unselfishness. What added to these great victories was

Jones's amateur status. He remained an amateur. He never turned professional. Most likely because his character insisted on giving to the game, never the reverse. This is one way of seeing Great Possession.

stages of possessing what is great

LINE 1 · A Great Golfer stays away from what is harmful. He doesn't even approach it. This is good game management.

LINE 2 · Great Golfers have equanimity. Steady your game.

LINE 3 · A Great Golfer shares what he has, for example, knowledge and comfort. An insecure and fearful golfer finds it difficult to give to others. Don't be selfish.

LINE 4 · A Great Golfer knows his limits. Don't try to match the game of others, as doing this could come from pride and envy. The Great Golfer also realizes that his talent may not come from just him.

LINE 5 · A Great Golfer knows dignity. This means quiet confidence in your game and character. It keeps the respect of your playing partners and golf community.

LINE 6 · To be a Great Golfer means to know what you are blessed with. It is up to you to figure out what it is. This absolutely guarantees a successful golf character.

15. MODESTY

simplicity, moderation, lack of pretension

Find the part of the game you pay too much attention to and give some of that attention to what you pay very little attention to in your game.

Modesty as far as the *Golf Ching* is concerned means to take from what has a lot and give to what has a little. This creates balance. So if you're pounding away with your driver on the range, you might consider practicing the short game. This is modesty.

This image is of Francis Ouimet and his caddie during his upset victory over Walter Travis and others. Francis was young and put more into his game than the others realized. He didn't look the part. He certainly wasn't overly involved in his image. He paid attention to what he needed to win and not what he looked like. Both Ouimet and his caddie look the model of what we classically think of as *modest* and innocent. What Ouimet had was balance in his entire game. Perhaps the other players leaned too heavily on their images. Perhaps Ouimet's innocence helped lead him to victory.

stages of modesty

LINE 1 · You are modest even regarding your modesty. Go ahead, play the game and don't let too much modesty keep you back or weaken you or your game.

LINE 2 · Modesty does not necessarily bring recognition to your game. It can just result in paying attention and completing small things.

LINE 3 · This type of modesty is for occasions when you have achieved something. You then must proceed to be unaffected and unassuming.

LINE 4 · In this form of modesty, seek no external reward or recognition from others just because you are behaving modestly. This means you play every part of the game in moderation for your own sake and interest. For you.

LINE 5 · This type of modesty is energetic and forceful. This type of modesty doesn't appear to be weak or holding back; it could go for the win. This type of modesty can even attack the game.

LINE 6 · Modesty at its strongest is evident to others. It is inspiring to them. Now that everything about your game is balanced there is neither too little or too much in any one area. You have achieved the ability to perceive and act with modesty in every aspect. It comes so naturally now that you are on the brink of enthusiasm.

16. ENTHUSIASM

repose, calm confidence, happiness

Enthusiasm comes from having confidence in your game.

Enthusiasm comes from having confidence in your game. Having confidence in your game comes from knowing you are acting correctly on the course. This means your swing mechanics and/or your course management. Both are the basic actions that form your game. When they are right, and you know they are right (i.e., putts begin to fall), confidence builds in these areas. Enthusiasm can be aroused. Generally, this kind of enthusiasm can be misguided. You can have too much enthusiasm and not enough confidence.

This image of enthusiasm is Lee Elder leaping after his eighteen-foot putt dropped to win a sudden-death play-off. Of course, this enthusiasm occurs in hindsight. The putt has already dropped. Elder has won. But this does build confidence that the actions taken, course and swing management, have been the right ones. And this leads to a kind of repose, which in turn leads to enthusiasm for your actions before you even play the next round.

stages of enthusiasm

LINE 1 · There is a type of enthusiasm for golf that comes from exhaustion. It's hard to be enthusiastic, so you arouse it. This isn't helpful. You don't believe you, others don't believe you.

LINE 2 · Keep your enthusiasm in check all during the round. Solid as a rock. Don't let your enthusiasm or that of others lead you astray from the calmness of your game.

LINE 3 · Again, be cautious of other players' enthusiasm as it may not be right for you. At the same time, is their enthusiasm something you yourself are enthusiastic about?

LINE 4 · This type of enthusiasm is so doubtless it not only wakes you up but others as well. Great rounds can be played with this type of confidence.

LINE 5 · Enthusiasm for your game is sometimes restrained by pressure. Performance pressure perhaps.

LINE 6 · After a while you will know what kind of enthusiasm is appropriate to your game. Act on it immediately, or don't.

17. FOLLOWING

gaining followers, aligning with, according with

Accept and follow what is good and right about the game and your character.

Following in golf is about following what is good and right beginning with the rules, sound swing principles, and a quiet acceptance of what the game hands you. By following this way, you'll lead. You set an example by following.

This image is of the crowd following Bobby Jones. Notice that some of them are almost racing. What are they really following? What they are following is what Jones was able to follow: good principles and good character. He virtually led others by following what was good and right. Others easily recognized this and followed along.

stages of following

LINE 1 ˙ Have a change of heart. Listen to other players or teachers. You're trying to get at the truth of your game.

LINE 2 ˙ Figure out what habit in your game is inferior and isn't working.

LINE 3 ˙ Be willing to drop what you've figured is inferior in your game (a cherished habit, perhaps), even if it's pleasurable or easy.

LINE 4 ˙ Make sure you follow what's good for your game. For example, don't follow flattery too closely. Sincerely follow what will make your game sound.

LINE 5 ˙ Have confidence in whatever or whomever you're following to better your game.

LINE 6 ˙ Know when to stop following something. It may have exhausted its use for you and your game. It may be time to follow your own initiative.

18. IMPROVEMENT

working on what has been spoiled, practice

Practice. Know how to practice.

It's time to practice. Some part of your game has been neglected. Or something needs to be corrected. This lesson suggests you use some time to practice in this way: deliberate to find which area needs work, spend three days to understand completely what you're doing wrong, spend a day practicing the correction, then be on the alert for three more days to make sure the old habit doesn't creep back into your corrective practice.

This image is of Arnold Palmer practicing sand shots as a young amateur. Landing in a bunker can spoil a hole, particularly if one is not sure how to play the lie. Here, Palmer works on what can potentially spoil a tournament for him.

stages of practice

LINE 1 · A golf game can fall apart because of habits that no longer work. A new habit must replace an old one. Find the old habit so you can respond to it.

LINE 2 · Work at finding the old habit. Persist. Be careful about being too accepting of the old habit. It holds your golf game back.

LINE 3 · When you're correcting an old habit, don't blame yourself. Don't be hard on yourself.

LINE 4 · Allowing a bad habit to continue rather than finding the correction will cause you to regret it. It will ruin your game.

LINE 5 · Old habits that no longer work should be called what they are: mistakes. But old habits die hard. Naming them a "mistake" helps. Know you're replacing an old habit with a proper one.

LINE 6 · After you learn the correct technique of a new habit, it's best to make it yours by practicing it in your own way.

19. APPROACH

advancing, drawing near, promotion, a good influence approaching

Accept your shot so that you may gather yourself together.
Always retain your equanimity. It's a good approach for every shot.

This lesson is about how you approach your game. The main principle to follow is "consistent acceptance of what your game and the golf conditions give you." This is the approach. It means: Whether the condition of your game is good or bad, you must keep your equanimity. Even if you accomplish something great, you keep your equanimity. Toward playing partners you remain patient. This lesson is also about what approaches you after having practiced long enough to see some reward (note the previous lesson was about practice). What will you do as success approaches you? "Keep my equanimity" is your response.

This image is of Arnold Palmer looking a putt over. Palmer's approach is evident: He is accepting the condition. He is collecting himself. He is thinking of nothing else but this approach and this putt. This now gives him an equanimity. This is the best way to approach every shot and every round.

stages of approach and advance

LINE 1 ' As your game improves, watch that you don't lose your composure. Don't lose your equanimity.

LINE 2 ' As you approach a successful round, watch for a slight tendency to leak.

LINE 3 ' You can become too enthusiastic about approaching the right way. This gives your game an unfavorable condition. It is a relapse and is careless.

LINE 4 ' The perfect approach is feeling and movement and equanimity all wrapped up in balance. Look for signs of this.

LINE 5 ' Add to your approach modesty and a willingness to correct your game. Your game then becomes very attractive. Others will want to contribute.

LINE 6 ' Add honesty and generosity to your game. This makes you a "great-hearted player." Palmer, for example, is a great-hearted player. And this is how he approaches.

20. CONTEMPLATION

observation, awareness, looking over

Take time to reflect. Reflect on your attitude.

This lesson is about what you bring to your awareness by contemplation and observation. It is time to practice a type of meditation: *reflecting on your game*. It is time to study and probe what you know about the game. The lines below make suggestions on some aspects of reflection.

This image is of Tommy Armour ("The Silver Scot"). The attitude he is in is clearly a contemplative one. Maybe he is waiting. Maybe this is time out for him. Possibly the round is over. In any case this is a pose that allows him to reflect on an aspect of his game: his mechanics, attitude, and philosophy.

stages of contemplation

LINE 1 · Begin contemplating your game. If you are an inexperienced player, any way you do this is fine. If you have been playing a while, what you observe about the game must serve to deepen your experience of it.

LINE 2 · Be aware of any insight about this game, even if it comes to you slowly, as if slipping through cracks in a door. Persist in checking this insight out.

LINE 3 · Contemplate *your* game. Nobody else's.

LINE 4 · It's time to decide what to do with your observations. Do they contain the right principles of golf? Are they important enough to pursue?

LINE 5 · Observe your attitude toward the game. Especially criticism or blame. Is there anything that needs to be altered?

LINE 6 · Could there ever be a time that you never blame yourself or others while playing golf? Being blameless, that is the supreme attitude.

21. BITING THROUGH

persistence, going through a barrier

Don't blame yourself or anything for getting into trouble.

This is about getting into and out of trouble. This lesson says to persist in troublesome shots only after ruminating and thinking things through. This, rather than trying to break through an obstacle immediately. Using force immediately is definitely out of the question. Only after thought and contemplation should you be vigorous and go forward. This applies to whether you are in danger or not.

This image is of Arnold Palmer determined to get through a large obstacle of trees. Palmer usually thunders through, whatever the obstacle, so what needs to be observed in this image is that he has thought about his plan, understands the consequences, and with clarity and intelligence vigorously persists in getting through.

stages of persistence

LINE 1 · In any situation where you have found trouble, don't blame yourself. It's temporary.

LINE 2 · When you drive off the fairway, you have left good principles of golf behind. You usually have plenty of anger. Just make the correction. Get back with the correct principles. It can be that easy.

LINE 3 · When you haven't learned the correct attitude in dealing with trouble (and you've found more), everything falls apart. There is almost hatred. Temper it or you'll poison all subsequent shots.

LINE 4 · This is the kind of trouble where you merely have to correct the situation. Just be determined and go forward.

LINE 5 · This kind of trouble breeds plans. Sometimes going ahead with these plans doesn't work. You haven't learned from before.

LINE 6 · This is a time when your judgment isn't good. You shouldn't trust it in dealing with trouble on the course. You'll have to listen better.

22. ELEGANCE

grace, public image, adornment

*The purpose of adornment is to draw the eye
toward what it graces: the beauty of self-acceptance.*

This lesson is about gracefulness, beauty of form, and refinement in whatever we do or say. The true professional makes the game look easy through grace and form by what he *doesn't* do. The game thus appears to be uncomplicated. This comes from the professional's enormous knowledge of the game. Outwardly, he adorns himself with an accepting attitude. This attitude is then adorned. This is the time to know what it is you are drawing attention to. What are you adorning?

This image is of Walter Hagen, the first professional to *look* professional. Here he is clothed in white, the symbol of simplicity, elegance, and clarity. He was the first professional allowed in the front door of the exclusive golf clubs at which tournaments were played. Although Hagen dressed the part, it is important to know *what* he was dressing: self-knowledge, simplicity, gentleness, and acceptance. He was dignified and charming. And his charm reflected substance.

stages of elegance

LINE 1 ‧ Don't assume you know everything about golf. This isn't dignity. Don't abandon the *unknowing* attitude.

LINE 2 ‧ Golf has traditions. And one of them is that golf ought to be a pleasant game. At this time, it's good form to keep a smile on your face to practice this tradition. See if this practice can mirror something truthful.

LINE 3 ‧ Don't let gracefulness alone carry your game. Arrogance can slip in. Golf is a game of making corrections. Keep your determination.

LINE 4 ‧ The gracefulness you now have should not be used for show. You may have good intentions, but forcing them isn't good. Use some modesty.

LINE 5 ‧ Your elegance and grace on the course need to be seen as gifts. If you feel the gift of your elegance is small, don't. It has value, and there is no disgrace.

LINE 6 ‧ A player—you perhaps—has a simple elegance.

23. PARTING

splitting apart, fracturing, peeling off

This is a time to be calm and allow your game to work itself out. Even if your game is falling apart and you seem unlucky, the better part of it will return.

This lesson has several slightly different meanings. The first meaning is that this is a time when your game is getting rid of hindrances. Another meaning is that you're losing what you think you have, such as a good game or a bad game (your game may simply be falling apart). These meanings carry with them the consoling counsel that nothing can really be done about your game now. You should just wait it out and not try to fix things. Parting is unavoidable and necessary.

This image is of a player framed between a tree with two trunks; the splitting of the tree is to remind you of the process of splitting apart, of parting. Whatever is parting from your game, do not fight it now.

stages of parting

LINE 1 ˙ You see a sign that your game is falling apart. This sign is clear. Withdraw from trying to fix it. See it as the rhythm of your game.

LINE 2 ˙ What is peeling off from your game is what shouldn't be there any longer, i.e., playing partners, friends, a course, a teacher, or habits. This is unsettling to your game.

LINE 3 ˙ What you had in your game has left. This is for the best.

LINE 4 ˙ Your game is down. Everything you have must be directed toward correcting your attitude toward your golf game.

LINE 5 ˙ Within an unlucky streak, there is the possibility of changing luck. This comes about from being with other players and letting their good attitudes affect you immediately.

LINE 6 ˙ Bad attitudes grow on bad attitudes. Do not let a bad attitude affect how you treat yourself or other players.

24. RETURN

the turning point, recovery, a new beginning

Vitality is trying to return to your game. Accept the changes you need to make. Note what you want to have return and what you don't.

This lesson suggests that the vitality of your game is trying to return. It is a new beginning from a time of not doing as well as you wanted to. It is suggesting that you can now take a fresh approach to your game: Let your game develop naturally and accept the changes in it that you need to make.

This image is of Ben Hogan hitting a recovery shot out of the sand. Every player is familiar with recovery shots: the shots that return you to the fairway or green. Hogan's return is symbolic: his recovery from a near death car accident, his surprising return to the height of professional golf, his game returning and finding a miraculous level.

stages of recovery and turning points

LINE 1 ⋅ Your game needs to make a return to the basics. Find what you've left behind.

LINE 2 ⋅ Consider that you've made an admirable turn in your game.

LINE 3 ⋅ At a time you are expecting your game to return, be careful that you don't expect too much too soon. It could put your game in danger.

LINE 4 ⋅ In order to make the potential return, go it alone. Do not let others distract you.

LINE 5 ⋅ You now hold a benevolent attitude toward *the* game and *your* game. This is what is now returning. This attitude can also be for other players or a course.

LINE 6 ⋅ Confusion can return to your game in the form of self-pity, depression, envy, or jealousy. Clear this away or it will expend energy best spent on your game.

25. INTEGRITY

the unexpected, innocence, honesty

*Notice how this game is always finding an untouched place in you. The
game is always finding your untouched spirit of delight.*

This lesson is about integrity. The Sanskrit root of this word comes
from *tag*, meaning "to touch." Children play tag, a game of touch. *Integ*
means "not touched." Integrity means untouchable. In golf, this can
refer to the untouchable strength of one's honesty and accountability.

A psychological definition goes like this: What cannot be touched or sullied in your game? Your delight and enjoyment of the game. Your ability to keep your delight constant and prolonged and intact is your integrity. So, integrity in golf does not have to be a painful standard. Instead, the integrity of your game is a prolonged and focused delight.

This double image shows the innocent and heartfelt reactions of Arnold Palmer: The reactions of someone who is playing the game as if for the first time. Even after fifty years of playing, he still has delight for the game that nothing can touch. That is integrity. This is the Palmer spirit.

stages of integrity

LINE 1 · Playing the game with innocence by knowing the unexpected lies in wait is a good way to go.

LINE 2 · Don't bank on the reward of your integrity. Your game exists *now*, not on what your integrity will get you in the future.

LINE 3 · The unexpected happens all right; perhaps it is an unexpected turnover in the game. Your gain may be another player's loss. What do you make of that?

LINE 4 · You play an honest game. Now is the time to persist at whatever level.

LINE 5 · Don't apply any untried shots in your game now. The unexpected may show up and it may not be what you hope for.

LINE 6 · To play shots that are innocent, fun, and wild would lead to playing golf in a blundering way. Now is not the time to be playing this kind of golf, even though you're sincere.

26. TAMING YOUR GREAT POWER

restraining the great, taming great powers, holding back

Stillness is the great nourisher. Use it to tame yourself while playing.

This lesson is about how to restrain the power in you and, in addition, restrain the powers of other players. Stillness is an effective tool against doing too much, being too aggressive, trying to use power when their isn't much, overplaying. Taming your great power means to contain yourself.

This image uses Bobby Jones as a symbol of *taming great power*. He was known as the "Great Bobby Jones." Jones was always even-tempered in play. Notice here Jones welcoming a fellow competitor in the match. There is a stillness of the moment, a taming of the moment, a meeting of the eyes and hands. It's as if Jones is saying, "This is all that is happening." In effect, this throws the other player. Jones is containing himself. The other player may not be.

stages of holding back

LINE 1 ˙ Your power is getting your game into trouble. The competition may be tempting you; it may be the course. Stop. Don't be at all aggressive.

LINE 2 ˙ This is when the wheels have fallen off your game. It's better to wait for your power to return. A vital connection is missing.

LINE 3 ˙ It's best to play defensively and keep your game safe.

LINE 4 ˙ Keep the cap on using too much force in your game. Train yourself to do this so your game is not in danger.

LINE 5 ˙ If you have any desire to play all out, nip it in the bud. What are the likely consequences of playing like that? Not good.

LINE 6 ˙ You'll know when you've tamed forces in you that could overwhelm your game: The power of your game will flow appropriately.

27. PROVIDING NOURISHMENT

wise counsel

Nourish yourself and others.

This lesson is about nourishment. If you find your game unnourishing, watch how you nourish other players. Look at the quality of your nourishment. Watch how players nourish themselves to get some ideas for yourself. Watch how other players nourish one another. This is a time to see the game as nourishing. If it isn't nourishing, find out what is missing.

This image is of Auld Da, a caddie at St. Andrews Old course in the late 1800s, selling lemon squash and ginger pop to Old Tom Morris on site. This picture reminds you to stay nourished during play. Nourishment is an important message throughout the *Golf Ching:* nourishment in the form of food, emotions, words, playing partners, and the course environment.

stages of nourishment

LINE 1 · Be dependent only on yourself and your own game for nourishment. Don't be dependent on anyone else. This could mean not envying other players.

LINE 2 · A player is again advised against abandoning himself to get nourishment. Don't try to get nourished by something that isn't right.

LINE 3 · Don't think you can do without nourishment. You'll lose sight of the fact that your game is connected to everything.

LINE 4 · Nourish yourself by watching players you admire.

LINE 5 · Although you don't have to do anything extreme to nourish yourself and your game, checking out other ways is all right.

LINE 6 · Ideally, you'll find the source of nourishment is your own good work on your game.

28. PRESSURE

excess, critical mass

The pressures of golf can be managed or they can be too much.
Don't add to them.

This lesson is about pressure. Your game is under pressure or you are pressuring your game. It makes playing ponderous. It's time to distribute the pressure that may be building up by being flexible. It is not the time to be aggressive in order to solve the pressure. Be gentle. You may be expecting too much from only one part of your game (e.g., scoring, performance). Try to have a more balanced game by paying attention to other aspects of it.

This image is of Dr. Cary Middlecoff bending in the middle over a missed putt. He is pressuring himself excessively. Not coincidentally,

Middlecoff was plagued by back problems later in his career, forcing him into early retirement.

stages of pressure

LINE 1 ᐧ If you're pressuring yourself to play well, be cautious. Don't rush. Give some attention to the details of the game.

LINE 2 ᐧ You have playing experience. You're under pressure. Try falling in love with a new attitude to use this experience to greater benefit.

LINE 3 ᐧ The pressure of the game is big now. Don't push ahead as you have been. Your game won't benefit.

LINE 4 ᐧ You'll overcome pressure by abiding by the correct principles of balance in your game. When you overcome this, don't think it all that important or you may backslide.

LINE 5 ᐧ Your experienced golf game has an attitude that is too different for it. This attitude may not last long. But it will be helpful for as long as it lasts.

LINE 6 ᐧ This kind of pressure in your game means you are in over your head. Maybe it's the compassion, expectation, a difficult course. Don't blame yourself.

29. THE ABYSS

danger, fearlessness

Find a way out of your own abyss first: frustration,
reckless abandon, anxiety, and despair. Then play golf.

This lesson tells you how to get through danger on the course. The
main suggestion is not to hit shots from frustration or despair. The idea
is to act a little more fearlessly, but not recklessly. This lesson applies
best when you consider the real danger in playing golf comes from
your own frustration, despair, anxiety, or recklessness. If you consider
this, then you can think of these emotions and attitudes as the abyss
inside you.

This image is of Ben Hogan hitting out of the water and onto the green. Hogan's ball had landed on the green, then spun back into the water. He was definitely miffed. He escaped from his own dangerous frustration before he attempted to escape the dangerous water. This is the way to do it.

stages of danger

LINE 1 · Your attitude is getting your game in danger. For some reason you're keeping it.

LINE 2 · Now your game is in danger. Don't try to make huge gains or improvements in your game now.

LINE 3 · You're attitude is quite bad (it may not be a time to play golf). Calm down. Absolutely pause before every shot.

LINE 4 · A player in a deep abyss generally gets help and advice from others. It is good to share the finer points of the game.

LINE 5 · If you cannot easily move from one attitude to another (at least this is some kind of movement), then wait. Have a little patience.

LINE 6 · The extent of danger in your golf is completely due to impatience. The less patience, the longer the danger.

30. BEAUTY

clarity, intelligence

Cling to the basic golf principles. Your golf game is dependent on them.
That's the beauty of the game.

The lesson here is beauty: knowing the basic golf principles and the rewards that come from adhering to them. Our golf game is totally dependent on knowing these basics. You can learn a lot about yourself by realizing how far you've veered from the basics of golf. The basics give your game clarity and can be practiced over and over. Stick with them, and don't leave them behind. That's the beauty of the game: basic principles.

This image is of Ben Hogan hitting his famous one-iron shot to the eighteenth green in the U.S. Open. This picture ranks as one of the most popular and beautiful golf shots ever filmed. Hogan's swing captured the perfect execution of golf principles. Whatever school of golf a player is from, he is sure to benefit from the beauty of Hogan's fundamental swing. One might say there is nothing there but the basics. They're beautiful.

stages of beauty

LINE 1 · Have respect for the basic principles of golf. Don't hurry in learning or reviewing them. Take it step by step.

LINE 2 · Practice the basics of this game in a *medium* manner. No need to get excessive or go overboard. Enjoy the rewards.

LINE 3 · The rewards of practicing the basics do not last forever. Rewards set like the sun. Let your game rise and fall as you adhere to the basics.

LINE 4 · A sudden insight, a sudden improvement, a sudden beauty in your game can flare up, then disappear abruptly before you can count on it.

LINE 5 · It's difficult learning and relearning the basics. It's frustrating. Emotional.

LINE 6 · Accept that there are always unwanted habits trying to creep in. Be *vigorous,* and keep an eye on these habits as you review the basics.

31. WOOING

influence, persuasion, attraction, sensation

If you want to influence your game successfully, you must maintain a strong center. Influencing your game is almost like wooing it.

This lesson is about what influences you as a player and in turn how you influence your game. Whatever is influencing you is felt in your body. It is felt in your form and your swing. These influences become sensations, which, in turn, you act on and put into your game. Influences come and go. But you must always maintain a strong, quiet center in your body to take advantage of the good influences and to ward off the bad.

This image is of Louise Suggs being influenced by her putt. It may seem on first glance that she is using her body English to persuade her putt to drop. Both are influencing each other: The ball is leading her into this almost wooing posture, and at the same time she believes this position might help her cause.

stages of attraction and influence

LINE 1 · Something is beginning to influence your game. Don't rush.

LINE 2 · You don't understand what is influencing your play. Don't let it influence you until you know and understand it.

LINE 3 · Find what you're clinging to in this game that is inferior: theories, playing partners, teachers, a previous round. Some are not good influences.

LINE 4 · Your playing form is a little off balance and agitated. Get rid of the ambition and be a little more still.

LINE 5 · You're trying to exert your will in your game. It's a good time for that. It's not quite there, but it's still a good time.

LINE 6 · You're talking about your game too much.

32. THE LONG ENDURING

duration, continuity, maturity

You can play this game your entire life.
Endure and see your life unfold as you play.

This lesson is about the long enduring. You can play this game your entire life. How will you do it? What will give your game continuity? What is the spirit behind it? It can be adaptability, love, understanding, devotion, and persistence.

This image is of Old Tom Morris. Tom Morris was *the* famous resident at St. Andrews: a four-time British Open champion, clubmaker, golf course architect, and morning bather in the freezing waters of the East Bay. Last but not least, his renown was for golfing righteousness: *"Play the ball as it lies. Don't touch the ball with anything but a club until it's holed out. Abide by the spirit of the game."* He played golf into his eighties. Old Tom Morris is the model of the long enduring in golf.

stages of long enduring

LINE 1 ᐧ Skillful golf is created slowly and carefully. Don't try to accomplish too much, too soon. If your game is to endure, let it grow at its own pace.

LINE 2 ᐧ If you have regrets about your game, let them disappear.

LINE 3 ᐧ Inconsistency in your game and you as a player will corrupt your game. Your game will not endure this way. Others will not endure you as a player. Get centered.

LINE 4 ᐧ You're seeking something for your game, but in the wrong place. It isn't appropriate for your game enduring.

LINE 5 ᐧ Conforming and thereby losing your individuality right now is not a good way to give your game endurance and continuity. Don't lose your own game.

LINE 6 ᐧ Take care that your game does not become restless or agitated. This ruins the game's continuity.

33. RETREAT

withdrawal, yielding, retiring

This is the time of retreat. It is a time for being still.
A time for only small improvements in your game.
Practice withdrawing the forcefulness and emotion you have invested.

This lesson of retreat suggests that this is the time to realize your golf game waxes and wanes. Much of golf is using wise restraint, e.g., getting through the woods, hitting long shots over water, going directly at the pin. For the good of your game as a whole, it is time to withdraw expectations; practice withdrawing the forcefulness and emotion you have invested. This isn't a time to push ahead or to be aggressive. Maybe there is a seasonal change; maybe the rhythms in your own life are changing. These are immovable rhythms. Retreat from them.

This image is of an amateur golfer hitting away from the hole and into a wall. This player has found she can't address the ball normally to strike it. In order to advance toward the hole, she has to go backward and off the wall. This is going backward to go forward, retreating in order to advance, making only a small advance. This idea applies to the whole of your game.

stages of retreat

LINE 1 · Don't seek any goals in your game right now. Regarding attitudes, emotions, and other energies: do not use less of them now or use more. Stay steady. Wait. Retreat from wavering.

LINE 2 · With great determination find something very small to improve in your game. This is all that can be accomplished with your great determination. Retreat from making large accomplishments.

LINE 3 · Stop struggling emotionally with your game. Retreat from any regret, insecurity, or self-doubt.

LINE 4 · Even if you don't want to withdraw something from your game, if not from the game entirely right now, do it. And don't let it bother you.

LINE 5 · Be firm in your decision to withdraw (whatever you're withdrawing). Don't be seduced into using it again.

LINE 6 · When you withdraw your energies a bit in this game, it's best to do it cheerfully. Everybody benefits then.

34. POWER OF THE GREAT

great power, vigor

Find and wield power from your game only.

This lesson is about how to direct a great concentration of power. It is also about finding the heart of *your* game. As a golfer you *will* find your own game. Your own game gives you a sense of great power. If you don't feel this power, you may be relying on someone else's game, a game someone else has chosen for you, not your own path.

This image is of Bobby Jones. He was known as the "Great Bobby Jones." Jones gained his title not only from his many victories and classical swing but also because of his amateur status. The true amateur plays the sport out of love for the sport. And this is what people recognized. Jones embodied the greatest power, love of the game. He played a game of the heart: always modest, honest, patient, and persistent.

stages of great power

LINE 1 · Heartfelt power is just emerging in your game. Just remain honest and confident. Don't wield power you don't have.

LINE 2 · Be patient and persistent as the power in your game emerges.

LINE 3 · Absolutely refrain from using overt power in your game. It will only lead to entanglement down the road.

LINE 4 · Now is the time to use power. The wheels begin to turn for *your* game. Persist in the direction *you're* going.

LINE 5 · By finding *your* game, difficulties you've been experiencing will fall away. You can now exercise your game more freely.

LINE 6 · Your game has some difficulty. Don't struggle. Just wait for the difficulty to pass.

35. PROGRESS

succeeding, making headway

This is a time when you can make easy progress.
Take advantage of it. Don't sabotage your game with harshness.

This lesson is about progress, and it suggests you *are* making progress in your game. The type of progress referred to here is the type that comes easily, like the natural growth of a plant pushing upward. Progress in your game can be made by seeing the obstacles of off-attitudes, unwieldy emotions, and distracting thoughts as simple hindrances. By being a fluid player you simply have the insight to see them clearly and ignore them.

This image is of Bobby Jones as a boy and as an adult player. This is simply to show the progress that can be almost unavoidable over the years of practicing and playing. It is simple, uninterfered with, fluid progress.

stages of progress

LINE 1 · If you don't have confidence in your game, just remain cheerful. This is remaining fluid.

LINE 2 · You're making progress in your game, but you're not that happy about it. Let someone bring some cheer to your progress.

LINE 3 · Everything in you as a player is in unison to get better. There's no regret for the game you leave behind. Don't moan about your game.

LINE 4 · The progress in your game isn't that great. You're just being frenetic and trying to get somewhere too fast. Calm down.

LINE 5 · Don't try to know how much progress you've gained or lost in your game. Don't take either way to heart. Just devote yourself to playing better.

LINE 6 · Don't use any harshness as you try to make progress. Beware of too much aggression as well. Sometimes it isn't clear how to get better as a player.

36. DARKENING OF THE LIGHT

hiding light, indirect devotion

Don't engage yourself with negative attitudes inside or surrounding you.
Let these influences pass, and pay attention to your own will.

This lesson is about your golf game darkening. You might find your game darkening; it may be your score, your interest in the game, attitude, physical energy, or devotion. Any of these may be darkened. Don't fight it. Remain somewhat detached from what is overshadowing your game. Consider this a gestation time. Darkening can be used as a strategy to survive a round. It can be a way to hide your reserves; this is something competitive golfers sometimes do. The darkening is part of a larger cycle.

This image is of a dark Ben Hogan (although he finished well in this tournament). Hogan actually was tired during this round. He is not showing any inner light, any competitive fierceness, because of his fatigue. And he was not one to fight it. He knew better. But he was fast at work inside himself, planning his next shot as he walked. This illustrates hiding one's intelligence and strength and working in silence. It shows not trying to battle fatigue. His was a purposeful acceptance of darkening of the light.

stages of darkening of the light

LINE 1 · Keep your focus. This is a time to stay willfully on track no matter what.

LINE 2 · Your resources are not available to you as they normally are. Don't give it any thought. Persist in your game. It will help your game to help other players with theirs.

LINE 3 · After finding out what is weakening your game, don't be so eager to get rid of this habit (or whatever it is). It may be the glue holding your game together.

LINE 4 · If you probe deeper into your game and find habits you don't like, you might find you can't do anything about them. It's best not to fight it.

LINE 5 · If you are experiencing your game as tyrannical, it can hurt. Keep a small light of persistence lit inside yourself. It's a dark game now.

LINE 6 · What cannot be stressed enough is that dark moments and periods of golf go up and down, taking you with them. If you've enjoyed great heights of playing, perhaps experiencing sinking low is part of this large pattern.

37. THE FAMILY

intimate association, a group, bonding

Your game is important to other players. You're part of the golf community.

This lesson is about the reasons golf communities exist: for intimacy, love, bonding, assistance, survival, growth, and mutual support. The golf community is there to follow your life. Your association with your group has advantages for all players in the golf community. This is a time to demonstrate your higher feelings toward your golf community: natural affections, openness, and generosity.

This image is of John Reid, early enthusiast of American golf, his sons, and friends at what is today the oldest continuously existing golf club in America. Built on an apple orchard in Yonkers, New York, he called it the St. Andrews Golf Club, presumably after the old club in Scotland.

In this picture, Reid is teaching his sons to caddy and gaining his friends' interest to take up the sport. Notice the respectful distance everyone keeps from one another. Intimate, yet not suffocating.

stages of the family

LINE 1 · There are no regrets about the players you play with or the club where you play. It is a safe group.

LINE 2 · It's good for your golf community that you nourish yourself. Choose food, thoughts, ideas, beliefs that feed you. Don't try to influence other players. This is just for you.

LINE 3 · In all golf communities, tempers flare up. This happens. And it's over. But constant mockery in the community isn't good for anyone. Be on the watch for this tone. It destroys intimacy.

LINE 4 · It's good to realize from time to time your role in your golf community. And it's good to affirm that you have a place in it and are valuable.

LINE 5 · It's good to realize what effect you have on other players. Every time you play with others it's beneficial to know there is a human bond. Others appreciate your part in it.

LINE 6 · Realize that other players enjoy your company and your game. They enjoy your form of confidence in yourself and in them. In some way, shape, or form, your sincerity helps other players.

38. OPPOSITION

estrangement, alienation

Handle opposing viewpoints, attitudes, opinions, and positions from other players and within yourself with tact and generosity. It helps bridge the gap.

This lesson is about any kind of opposition, whether it is with another player or within yourself. The feeling of alienation, estrangement, and opposition usually comes about when a player's needs are not met, when there is a rift, when there is a discrepancy between what a player feels he should obtain and what is actually possible.

This image shows Arnold Palmer and Jack Nicklaus in heated contention. The opposition and competition between these two players always brought richness to the game. The state troopers escorting the players can be seen as symbolic of the need to regulate opposition; they are making sure neither player becomes alienated or estranged.

stages of opposition

LINE 1 · Inevitably, you're going to play either with someone you don't like or play a golf game (yours) you don't like. Both can be *alienating*. Communicate with the unpleasant player, and don't go chasing after your game.

LINE 2 · You may be estranged from your game. It's exactly at times like this that you accidentally get it back.

LINE 3 · You may feel that you've worked enough at your game but are still distressed, almost humiliated. It doesn't seem worth it, but it is.

LINE 4 · If you've been feeling alienated from your usual game or companions, what you've been working for comes through.

LINE 5 · If you've had regret in your golf game, it's disappearing so you can go forward. Regret has colored your game unproductively.

LINE 6 · When you first feel alienated from your game, you tend to take it to heart and blame the game. The game is not trying to deplete you. A setback is now, instead, a good sign.

39. OBSTRUCTION

barrier, obstacles, trouble

*The purpose of an obstruction is to give you pause so you
can gather your resources and find a solution. Be calm and fearless.*

This lesson is about encountering obstacles in the way of progress: obstacles in the game that make action and progress difficult, encountering thoughts and emotions that stop you from progressing in your game. The solution to such situations is to keep calm while being fearless. Through being observant and fearless, solutions appear and the time to act emerges. It means not being harsh. It means being responsive to trouble openly, almost warmly. It's always best to pause until your inner resources build so you can face whatever obstacle there is.

This image is of Arnold Palmer's stance being obstructed by a tree. This is an obvious barrier to progress as Palmer would like to know it. How he deals with it is firmly, clearly, and in accepting the only way possible: wrapping himself around the obstacle.

stages of barriers

LINE 1 · The type of obstacle you have in your golf game is acting too quickly. Your game requires waiting. Wait first.

LINE 2 · Don't blame yourself for whatever obstacles you experience in your game. The kind of obstacles you keep having are external and aren't a reflection of your desire.

LINE 3 · The kind of obstacles you have require you to turn back to an equanimity, an evenness of action.

LINE 4 · It's still difficult to go forward with the kind of obstacles impeding you. Whether they are emotion or thought, they are beginning to recede.

LINE 5 · Whatever obstacles you encounter, think of the proper principles involved with them as friends. Think of friends arriving to help.

LINE 6 · With this kind of obstacle, always take the high road. That is, ask yourself or another player, "What's the best thing to do here?"

40. DELIVERANCE

letting go, eliminating obstacles

A change in attitude delivers a new game to you.

This lesson is about letting go and deliverance. Often in golf, when a player hits a good shot, it releases him from tension. This tension almost always comes from condemning, criticizing, and worrying about past shots and expectations of future shots. One good shot suddenly delivers the player onto the right path, where he becomes free from this tension. The responsibility, then, is to keep up this delivered attitude and freedom. For now, the practice is to forgive mistakes and to correct them as best you can so you can play golf.

This image is of Jack Nicklaus looking skyward after sinking a lengthy putt. Nicklaus is looking up as if he has let go of tension and worry, is thanking his lucky stars, and is forgiving himself for ever having any doubts. He has suddenly been released from the tension of expectation.

stages of deliverance

LINE 1 · Start fresh and assume you've not made any mistakes. You're playing at your own level.

LINE 2 · Arm your golf game with this attitude (*"What mistakes?"*). It kills three birds with one stone: condemning, criticizing, and worrying.

LINE 3 · Your golf game has a little too much pride in it. This is not where deliverance is supposed to lead. You'll rob yourself of benefits.

LINE 4 · Beware of your golf game being dependent on old friends like worry and criticism. A new friend in which you can put your trust in will arrive. Faith, perhaps.

LINE 5 · Now is the time actively to stop habits you know are keeping you from this game. This is the game of *this is the only shot*.

LINE 6 · First, shot by shot, kill any attitude that would fail to deliver you to *this is the only shot*.

41. DECREASE

loss, reduction

Golf has loss and gain. Loss and gain are simply changes.
They are neither good nor bad. It is how we perceive them that matters.

This lesson is about loss and your response to it. Loss always seems unfortunate. The loss conveyed here is the type of loss that leads to gain and increase. You must remain confident in your abilities and be confident that the losses described here will turn to gain. This is a time to conserve your resources, a time to meet your needs rather than desires and grander expectations; it is not a time to be excessive. It is a time to place your attention correctly on loss and strategically to turn it to gain.

The image is of Arnold Palmer at a loss. It is a graphic example that shows how he deals with it: He is moving with it. He's become smaller, decreasing himself. This is symbolic of accepting decrease. Nothing more, nothing less. Everyone in the gallery loves the way Palmer handles loss. It's amazing how his attitude has been his fortune.

stages of loss

LINE 1 · Moving quickly from shot to shot is admirable, but it can harm your game. You may think it helps others to move things along, but it takes away from your game.

LINE 2 · As long as you keep the dignity of your game, you'll help the game of others. This means increasing the game for others' betterment without lessening yours.

LINE 3 · It's time to lose whatever is complicating your game: You have either too many swing thoughts, attitudes, teachers, or partners. Lose one. Use one.

LINE 4 · Sometimes it helps to lose some bad golf habits. Start by losing a little sophistication and letting in some innocence.

LINE 5 · You'll help your golf game enormously by perceiving loss correctly. It turns the tide to gain.

LINE 6 · As you gain a better game, it is possible that it is not at the expense of others. Others don't lose. This is a marker of being on the right track.

42. INCREASE

gain, expansion, benefit

You can prolong a good streak by making sure others benefit from your game. Increase what you find admirable.

This lesson is about what to do during a time your golf game is growing quickly. Something about it is on the increase: improvement, winning, enjoyment, or any benefit you can think of. In a period of expansion and increase, you want to insure you take advantage of it. You do this by imitating and increasing what you find admirable and by making sure others benefit as well.

This image is of Arnold Palmer celebrating. Notice how Palmer seems well aware of his gallery and how his increase is theirs as well. This is another of Palmer's gifts: sharing his good fortune.

stages of increase

LINE 1 ˙ This is as good a time as any to add vigorously something you find admirable to your game.

LINE 2 ˙ Increase your persistence in doing what you believe is right for your game.

LINE 3 ˙ Your game can benefit from the difficulty, effort, or experience of another player. Not to worry. His difficulty was not your fault.

LINE 4 ˙ Keep a balanced attitude toward your game. You can do this by talking about your game with other players. This helps prolong whatever is benefiting your game.

LINE 5 ˙ Simply have confidence in your game as it is. Do not ask questions of teachers and other players. Make sure you extend your kindness to other players.

LINE 6 ˙ Warning: If your game doesn't help other players, it invites a downturn. Your game must somehow benefit other players. Do not lose this perspective.

43.   BREAKTHROUGH

determination, decision

Be decisive about habits you are changing, and stay with them.

This lesson is about the determination to stay with good habits, whether they are swing mechanics or attitude, and the breakthrough that comes from doing it. Breakthroughs in your game are very important because they mean you've gotten rid of some hindrances and are playing more freely.

This image is of a player who looks as if he's broken through the sound barrier. It is not a picture-perfect finish, but it is a picture of determination. This picture is symbolic of an aspect of this lesson: Be tenacious in sticking with your resolve.

stages of breakthrough

LINE 1 · You may not be equal to the game you expect of yourself. You may start out well, but your resolve may falter. Your resolve is still young.

LINE 2 · If you are armed with a good basic knowledge of your game, any fears you have are just mere disturbances.

LINE 3 · Don't make an outward show of strength to prove your determination. Especially if you don't feel strong. There is murmuring inside you challenging your resoluteness.

LINE 4 · You're trying to accomplish something in your golf game, but the circumstances aren't right. You may find this hard to believe.

LINE 5 · Whatever your goal in golf (which must be realistic), be tenacious.

LINE 6 · A player needs help in his game but is not asking for it. If it is you, ask. It benefits players to help and you to be helped.

44. CONTACT

coming to meet, meeting

The impact area is the most important part of your swing.
Making flush contact is one of the major impulses to play golf.

This lesson is about our many attempts and strategies for making contact with the golf ball. Impact and the impact area are the most important parts of the golf swing. Everything you do in your swing comes to meet this moment. If you meet the ball flush, the reverberation that is felt in your body is one of the major impulses to play golf. This is one of the few lessons that specifically addresses an area of swing mechanics.

This image is of Bobby Jones right before impact. His is one of the most classical and rhythmical swing patterns of all time. Here, every part of his pattern is involved in squaring the face of the club to make the contact he wants.

stages of contact

LINE 1 ᛫ You're weak in the hitting area. You're having trouble making contact. You've got the correct swing path. It's just a little inconsistent.

LINE 2 ᛫ You know what the faults and fixes of making solid contact are. You're advised to check this out with other players and teachers. This is another way of making contact.

LINE 3 ᛫ You're still not making the contact you would like. Golf is sometimes a game of misses. If you're aligned toward your target correctly, you can miss the ball straight. Even so, it's painful not making contact.

LINE 4 ᛫ You simply have no idea why you're not making contact. You don't seem to have access to what you know. This may be spreading to the way you make contact with other players.

LINE 5 ᛫ Protect the pattern and rhythm of your swing so that it can reach full development of squareness and club-head speed at contact.

LINE 6 ᛫ You may think you should make flush contact with the ball all the time. You don't need to. Don't think this way right now. It leads to exhaustion and regret.

45. GATHERING TOGETHER

massing, assembling

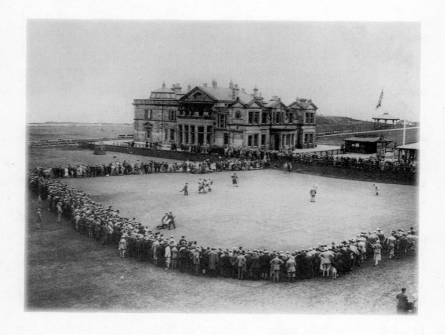

*Being part of a golf community allows you
to inspire each other and share in a collective joy.*

This lesson is about gathering together. When a group of golf enthusiasts are gathered together, there is almost a natural unity. You can find this at most professional golf tournaments. It is always important to gather together in order to remind yourself of what is possible in the game: joy and inspiration. Both these qualities give everyone confidence in their own games. Take some time to be part of a group that watches good players.

This image is of a group gathered around the massive last green at the Royal and Ancient Golf Club of St. Andrews. There is almost a group reflectiveness, as if this were a religious ceremony. Notice, too, this green has room for everyone gathered. Everyone is gathered to be collectively inspired and to feel he belongs to this inspiration.

stages of gathering together

LINE 1 · A player should actively be enjoying the game with others. It can be difficult when the confidence in your game comes and goes.

LINE 2 · Let yourself be drawn toward other players who are attractive to play with or to learn from.

LINE 3 · Sometimes a group of players you'd like to be a part of seems closed to you. Don't press it. You don't want to be denied.

LINE 4 · Playing your own game and gathering players around you for the sake of gathering a group is a good thing to pursue.

LINE 5 · Any golf group that you are a part of either by joining or organizing should be having a good time. Every last player.

LINE 6 · There is always a player who wants to belong but whose desire is overlooked. Sometimes this causes some suffering until his desire is aired.

46. PUSHING UPWARD

advancing, ascending

*Now is the time to advance the level of your game by
applying steadiness of will. Take advantage of this time.*

This lesson is about the steadiness of your will, your will to make
progress from whatever level you are playing at. It suggests that to
push upward you must be continuous and steady. The result is that
your game will rise from obscurity to your having more power and influence over it. It's probably a good thing to see a teacher so your
progress remains unimpeded. The *Golf Ching* highly values steadiness.

This image is of Bobby Jones hitting a short pitch. His club pointing upward in the finish position is symbolic of your growing game, your steady will to improve, pushing upward, timing.

stages of advancing

LINE 1 ⋅ This is a good time to push to move up a level in your game. You've got enough confidence. Look to see who is welcoming your efforts.

LINE 2 ⋅ Your form is not ideal; it is not picture-perfect. It may seem you don't fit into the level you're trying to reach. Yet it doesn't matter. Your faith matters more.

LINE 3 ⋅ There is nothing impeding your improvement. Take advantage of this. You don't know how long this can last.

LINE 4 ⋅ Sacrifice playing for a while. Traditional practice will serve your game well.

LINE 5 ⋅ Progress is made by consistent effort. Little by little you will see an effect on your game.

LINE 6 ⋅ Do not try to advance your game blindly or impulsively. Do what is best for your game, and make it consistent.

47. EXHAUSTION

weariness, distressed

Awareness of weariness is different from the weariness itself.
Your awareness will allow your game to progress.

This lesson is about exhaustion. It is about the weariness you feel as a player when your game does not grow and improve. This is why the game seems to become oppressive after a while and life seems to run out of you. This is a time to keep playing and not give up. It's not a time to explain to others how weary you are. It is a time to continue to try to find a way through the fatigue. Know that the awareness of weariness is different from the weariness itself. It allows you to continue and your game to grow.

This image is of a nearly fainting Ken Venturi during the 1964 U.S. Open. He has no memory of beginning the final round in hundred-degree heat. He became dehydrated and shook walking down the fairways. And he won. This is symbolic of your game distressing you *in any way*. It leads to exhaustion, yet there is a way through it.

stages of exhaustion

LINE 1 ⸱ You're looking for nourishment where there isn't any. You're on the wrong track.

LINE 2 ⸱ You're nourishing yourself and your game, but still you're exhausted. Being considerate might help now. See this in the form of an offering.

LINE 3 ⸱ What you're pursuing in your game cannot nourish or sustain you. You're leaning on the wrong principles. This exhausts you.

LINE 4 ⸱ Everything you need to play well is in place, but still your progress is slow. This can be exhausting. You'll get there, though.

LINE 5 ⸱ If you've set a goal for your game, difficulty in attaining it can be tiring. Other players can be tiring to you if you compare yourself. Instead, remain buoyant.

LINE 6 ⸱ Exhaustion creeps into your game if you regret shots you haven't even made. Resolve to get a grasp on your game and deal with what tires you.

48. THE WELL

the source, nourishment

You can change your game all you want, but nothing replaces the correct principles. They're an inexhaustible source of improvement and reward.

This lesson is about the source and wellspring of good golf: correct principles. You can change your game all you want, but the principles remain the same. You cannot move them or change them. Too often, players expect their games to reflect changes they've made in their games without realizing the importance of irreplaceable principles.

This image is of Ben Hogan retrieving his ball from the hole. This is symbolic of drawing cool water from a well; in golf, it means drawing up and being nourished by immovable golf principles. A player can then draw pleasure and rewards from the game. Hogan, the master of correct principles, always drew from his well of clear principles.

stages of nourishment

LINE 1 · Your golf basics have gone murky and are unclear. If you allow this to distress and shatter your game, other players will find it hard to help. Clear up the basics.

LINE 2 · Correct principles are leaking out. Not only that, but incorrect principles are leaking in.

LINE 3 · You've sorted out the basics but aren't using them as you might. Your game is ready to use. You're not making the most of it.

LINE 4 · This is a time when you're trying to repair your game. This actually helps other players as well.

LINE 5 · This is a time the correct golf principles are in your game. You've reached down correctly.

LINE 6 · You have access to correct golf principles. Nothing is hindering you in practicing and applying them.

49. REVOLUTION

change, renovation

You will always be trying to change your game.
It's only when the time is right and whatever changes you've
made are complete that your game succeeds. Then your worry disappears.

This lesson suggests that a set of conditions in your game is passing away in favor of better ones coming along, for instance, mechanics, playing partners, courses, scoring, or attitudes.

This image is of Arnold Palmer in his revolving finish, symbolic of the revolution he brought to the game. The game completely and swiftly changed after Palmer came on the scene: He brought golf to the masses. This, in turn, is symbolic of your game being ripe for some form of renovation.

stages of renovation

LINE 1 · Use some restraint in making changes in your game. Only make a change when you're sure it needs to be done.

LINE 2 · If, after you run through the basics, there is no improvement, then and only then should you think of renovating your game. Don't hurry.

LINE 3 · At this time, when you're constantly getting the same feedback on your game, listen and do something about it.

LINE 4 · Do not worry about or regret the way you have been playing. This will free you up to make fundamental changes in your game.

LINE 5 · You're about to make fundamental changes in your game. Be clear and confident about them.

LINE 6 · A proper change in your game at this time has a beauty and elegance to it.

50. THE VESSEL

the cauldron, the sacred cup

*See some of your actions as a way to reconnect to qualities
in golf you may be missing. These actions become small rituals to
remember the love, beauty, and magic of the game, thus filling the vessel.*

This lesson suggests you do something about finding and connecting
to the spirit of golf in some ritualized fashion. Whatever *quality* you
originally found in the game needs to be constantly connected to. For
some it is their *love* of the game, others find it is *beauty*, still others

magic. It is time to view some of your actions as an attempt to reconnect to these qualities, which the vessel of the game holds.

This image is of Walter Hagen and his teammates handling the Ryder Cup. It looks as if the cup is a sacred vessel the way he is handling it with others looking on. This image is symbolic of renewing the spirit of your golf game: *the quality of your relationship to it.* It is this quality that really nourishes.

stages of reward

LINE 1 ⋅ Venting about your game can be viewed as a simple action to get rid of inferior thoughts and feelings. What gets aired out has been standing in the way of a quality missing in your golf.

LINE 2 ⋅ Your game is solid because it contains qualities even others envy. You must realize that this is a real achievement.

LINE 3 ⋅ The qualities you bring to the game aren't recognized by other players, making it hard to be nourished. In time, you'll not need this recognition.

LINE 4 ⋅ You're paying too much attention to something outside *your* game. This causes the qualities of your game to spill out and get wasted. Reconnect.

LINE 5 ⋅ Approach your game in a simple way, with a little modesty and balance. This gives it strength.

LINE 6 ⋅ Prize whatever quality drives your game. It's valuable.

51. AROUSING

thunderous, shocking, eruption

There are always shocks to the game. Some golfers play in a perpetual state of shock and terror. Be prepared. Don't let the shocks that come poison you.

This lesson is about what happens to your game when you experience shocks and eruptions. Your game can suddenly change and sour. Your game going through an emotional time of anger or of arousal are examples of the effect of shock.

This image is of an angry Tommy Bolt. "Terrible Tommy" was always bursting with anger. This image is one of his milder poses. His club is not yet in the lake. Bolt's image serves as a reminder of the vitality of your game and how it can arouse you into many different emotional states. How you are prepared to traverse these inevitable states is of utmost importance.

stages of anger

LINE 1 · There are aspects of your game that are agitating and terrifying. These are exactly the parts of your game that can make you laugh.

LINE 2 · When you lose any part of your game suddenly, this is shocking. This is an instance when the correct measure is not to chase after it. Be philosophical, take the high road, and know it will come back.

LINE 3 · This kind of shock to your game points to times when you lose your composure and become distraught. This is good as it *wakes you up* a little and forces you to find the correct measures.

LINE 4 · There is a type of shock to your game that is followed by muddy thinking. What you must do here is just become aware of the confusion. Oddly enough, this allows better thinking to come around.

LINE 5 · Whenever shock after shock after shock happens in your game, you must be careful to stay centered and keep your faculties sharp. There is something going on that only you can attend to.

LINE 6 · There is a kind of shock to anyone's game that can take the breath away. It causes fear and trembling over every shot. The antidote: Wait it out by making sure the fear doesn't poison your body.

52. KEEPING STILL

calm contemplation, meditation

*Operating from a calm center sometimes means
quieting your body as you play. This might mean
swinging around a quieted body and not being so hasty.*

This lesson is about refraining from action. It refers to your spine and its posture. There are some schools of golf that advocate a "quiet body" in every shot. This can be a form of stillness and refraining from action. A good player's posture stays the same throughout the swing. The stilling of the spine allows your brain's messages to pass through and instruct your body.

This image is of Walter Hagen putting out on the final green. The stillness begins with Hagen and radiates throughout the crowd. This is symbolic of the effect that stillness can have on your entire game and the game of others when called upon.

stages of stillness

LINE 1 · Notice when you initiate your swing. Do not force-start it.

LINE 2 · You're hasty in your movements. This is disheartening to your game.

LINE 3 · In order to calm your game, your whole body must be quieted. But not so much that you stifle your game.

LINE 4 · Again, quiet your body by keeping the same posture aligned throughout your swing.

LINE 5 · Quiet your talk during your game. It's sometimes dangerous to talk too much. This calm will help you reflect. You'll find a better order to your words.

LINE 6 · This is a time to practice a type of stillness in your game that produces a general peace of mind; it is a sublime stillness from a calm center.

53. GRADUAL PROGRESS

slow and strong, developing

The way to go is gradual development.
That is how to persevere. Don't expect to grow faster than you should.

This lesson is about the steady development and gradual progress of your game *step by step*. The answer to moving along in an unchanging direction of progress and finding a game that will last is moving gradually. Do not rush improvement and try to achieve goals before their time.

This image is of Hogan crossing a bridge with his eyes looking downward. It was typical of Hogan to look downward as he played. This blocked out distractions and allowed him to attend to his shot making. This habit and the crossing of the bridge is symbolic of the *step-by-step* aspect of gradual progress.

stages of gradual progress

LINE 1 · Your game is gradually making progress. Your game may seem slightly unfamiliar, but consider that it is on new ground. Criticism abounds. *Some* is worth listening to.

LINE 2 · Your game has progressed further and is on more solid ground. Enjoy the pleasures of the game, and be with players who seem to be doing the same.

LINE 3 · Your game ought to develop naturally. You will jeopardize your game by forcing and struggling.

LINE 4 · To continue making gradual progress in your game, it is important to learn to adapt constantly.

LINE 5 · You may have reached a plateau that is part of progress in your game. It may seem that your game is almost sterile. Enjoy the plateau. It's time to pause and rest.

LINE 6 · To keep what you have developed in your game in order, develop some kind of ritual each time you play. This will serve to remind you of your progress.

54. UNION

transformation, the marrying maiden

*One can simply fall in love with this
game as if for the first time in order to transform it.*

This lesson is about finding whatever it is that will help transform your game. Normally, this is thought of as a change in your form. But it can be an attitude, swing thought, course strategy, another person, or anything. Oddly, it is not a good time for literally acting on these things but a time *not* to interfere with their workings.

This image is of Mrs. Tommy Armour waiting for her husband to finish tournament play. It is symbolic of one's game coming home to what completes it, needing to find what is missing, always being influenced and transformed.

stages of transformation

LINE 1 · This is the time a player unites with something that helps his game on its way. Its a good time to pursue whatever you sense this is.

LINE 2 · Sometimes the most remarkable changes in your golf form are unremarkable.

LINE 3 · One can simply fall in love with this game as if for the first time in order to transform it.

LINE 4 · It takes a while for changes in your form to take root. Postpone your expectations. Have a good relationship to time here.

LINE 5 · When you're changing your game, try not to compare it with that of others. Just attend to your game without making any big outward display.

LINE 6 · Sometimes making changes in your form is not substantial enough to really change anything at all. Your game just won't flow. So don't act on any goals.

55. ABUNDANCE

fullness, greatness

It is what you do with what you've got that fills out your game.
And it is time that what you've got makes you happy.

This lesson is about a player's game prospering. It is not a time to be sad or down but to focus on what you can attain with what you've got. One can start by filling the senses, by looking around the course and having a little gratitude and joy. Here is the caution: A player can easily fill up his game with darkness, and coming down always follows expanding. What is abundant in your game remains for you to observe and manage.

Look closely and you'll see this is an image of a one-armed player. This player was highly competitive and active on the circuit in his time. It is not his girth but his one arm that is the real symbol of an abundant game. Clearly this player focused on what he had, not what he didn't have. This is abundance.

stages of abundance

LINE 1 · Playing with players of equal skill is good for a period of time. Then, you must move on to expand your game.

LINE 2 · Sometimes what gets in the way of fulfilling your game is mistrusting what you know. Don't struggle against this, as it is part of becoming confident.

LINE 3 · When you think of yourself and your game as useless, you cease to be an able player. Terrible habits and a terrible player can often take center stage. If this is so, do not counter it. Let it ride itself out like an eclipse.

LINE 4 · Sometimes you cannot help your own game. You must rely on a player of equal skill or a player you resonate with to help you out.

LINE 5 · When what has been a cloud over your game lifts and you notice some of the signs, unexpected luck tends to start rolling.

LINE 6 · There are times when you play a good game or aspects of your game are fortunate, and you don't see it or them. If you also seal others out, the luxury of this game will certainly leave you. Don't alienate other players or yourself in pursuit of the *big* game.

56. WANDERING

traveling, searching

Golf is like wandering and traveling: A golfer
does not get rooted in any one situation. Treat the course as
if it were your host. All losses are simply signs to move on.

This lesson suggests that you consider yourself a guest and traveler on the course. Etiquette and conduct make you welcome. It suggests that you consider golf as travel: Stay out of trouble and move on quickly. This can apply to being in the rough, playing unfamiliar territory and courses, or being in new company.

This image is of Bobby Jones looking for his ball. Notice his care in moving the bush as he figures things out. It is a rule that the ball not be moved even accidentally. This care is also symbolic of the nature of the golfing wanderer: treading everywhere with care, knowing it is not your home and yet is everyone's home.

stages of wandering

LINE 1 ˙ Consider golf as travel. Do not get caught up in the game's little things. Don't let them absorb you and take up too much attention. You're traveling.

LINE 2 ˙ As a traveler, one finds out what one really owns. Playing golf is similar: find what you really own in your game, what makes you secure, and what gives your game its particular identity.

LINE 3 ˙ Your game can burn to the ground if you treat your course with a bad attitude. Remember that a golfer is a guest. Treat the course as if it were alive and it is your host.

LINE 4 ˙ There are times when players are not happy, even though they play well and all their needs are taken care of. Still, something is missing. This is the hallmark of a melancholic player: something is *always* missing.

LINE 5 ˙ One purpose of traveling is to experience loss as simply a way of moving on. Similarly in golf, experiencing any loss is simply the means to moving on.

LINE 6 ˙ Sometimes players are cruel to each other's play. Regret follows as they find the other person's play effects them, too. This is a sign that a player should pay attention to inappropriate behavior. Laughter, for example. Stay modest.

57. GENTLE

yielding, quiet, penetration

Establish a goal for your game, and
gently, persistently find your way toward it.

This lesson encourages being gentle and yielding and also having a goal for your game as you play. Being gentle, adaptable, and continuously working toward this goal has a lasting effect. Gradual effort makes the constant, gradual progress possible.

This image is of the young, gentle Francis Ouimet. Although he seems gentle enough, he had an unbending, clear, and defined goal: win. And he did so with the continuous yielding but penetrating effort. His loose and lanky pose is symbolic of this strategy.

stages of gentleness and yielding

LINE · Establish a goal for your game (or even one shot), and don't be hesitant about it. What is important is establishing a pattern of staying with your decision.

LINE 2 · When you establish a goal, it will call up hidden reasons, emotions, and inner antagonists to thwart you. They are only making rude suggestions. Counter them using whatever means necessary. Some players whistle.

LINE 3 · Don't exhaust yourself or your will by throwing yourself against obstacles and barriers in the way of your goal. It's humiliating and shows a lack of understanding of this lesson.

LINE 4 · Your thoughts and play in your game are effective since you can leave the regrets or remorse behind. This gives solid results.

LINE 5 · Keep persisting toward a goal you've laid out for your game. Eventually, there will be a turning point. Legend says this: Count three days before this point and three days after, then a concrete change in your game forms.

LINE 6 · Don't let your game crawl back to where it was. This is a time when you can lose what you've worked for if you yield to it.

58. JOYOUS

encouragement, pleasure

Joy comes from confidence and leads to encouragement.
Joy in golf comes from the inside, not from constant outside stimulation.

This lesson is about joy and pleasure that arise inside a player. This is not the same as trying to be amused and having your attention diverted. This type of joy comes from a stability inside the player that is strong and moves outward.

This image is of Jack Nicklaus sinking a very important putt. Notice his limbs going every which way. This is symbolic of the kind of joy that fills one full of lightness, wiping out all previous doubts, making room for encouragement. This joy then spreads to other players. Nicklaus's limbs are also symbolic of gentleness encasing great inner strength.

stages of joy

LINE 1 · Joy in golf can be had by remaining quiet and self-contained. Keeping the game simple so a player can practice this is important.

LINE 2 · Joy in golf can come from confidence and sincerity. Abandoning other players who have another agenda helps. Any tinge of remorse or regret should be noticed, then lost, to enjoy the pleasure of the game.

LINE 3 · Expecting pleasure only, a player may miss something important. This excessive devotion to the pleasures of the game may show a player to be empty inside.

LINE 4 · A lot of deliberating and reflecting can make a player restless. It is uncomfortable and wrecks the game's pleasures. Sometimes being too passionate about the game does this.

LINE 5 · Having blind faith in your game in order to mimic joy is not good golf. Parts of your game may be disintegrating. Be attentive to your game so that it does not crumble.

LINE 6 · The type of joy you're experiencing from your game is such an allure that *you* can be swept aside.

59. DISPERSING

dissolving, disintegrating

Leave any trouble shot or troubling attitude
with gentleness and refinement. Don't let it back in.

This lesson is about your game dispersing something unwanted in order to let in something better. This can refer to leaving the rough or a bad mental place. The strategy required is gentleness. When you're in specific situations that remind you of this, your swing needs to be finessed and refined to set up the next shot or attitude and help dispel anything troubling your game. Every trouble shot needs to be seen this way, and every troubling attitude needs to be noticed to leave it behind.

This image is of Arnold Palmer finessing his way out of a sandtrap. The sand flying is symbolic of dispersing and scattering the past by using gentleness and finesse. The trap can be seen as symbolic of leaving a sad place.

stages of dispersing

LINE 1 ' Leave all trouble quickly by taking the shortest route (hazards, rough, attitudes, other players) with strength and assuredness.

LINE 2 ' Something is leaving your game (dissolving) and you need to rely on what you know supports you. Play it safe while this dissolving takes place and you'll have no regrets.

LINE 3 ' When your game is in difficulty, it is time to forget about yourself completely. Put yourself away and give yourself over to the game.

LINE 4 ' When you're working toward the general welfare of the game, your ties to a group may have to disperse. This can be playing partners, course, playing time, or a group of old habits, patterns, and theories.

LINE 5 ' Sometimes the reason for your game dissolving is that a new passionate organizing principle is taking place. A major insight, perhaps. You'll know this because you'll tell everybody.

LINE 6 ' When something unwanted has left your game, it can seem as if you're wounded if you allow it back. Keep old associations at a distance.

60. LIMITATION

restraint, containment

Always know the limits of your game.
Know when to use them and when to exceed them.

This lesson is about how to use the strategy of limitation and restraint. Basically, using restraint is a nuisance. But this lesson is suggesting that sometimes the best way to play golf is *not* to do what you would normally and habitually do. It is about economy of movement, being efficient, and setting and knowing boundaries. It can be very effective.

This image serves as a reminder of restraint. Clearly there is a severe limitation here. A player must not swing or play as he normally would. A degree of restraint is called for or there will be consequences of the highest order.

stages of limitation

LINE 1 ⋅ If you're up against a desire to do something magnanimous in your game, now is the time to keep your swing quiet and contain yourself.

LINE 2 ⋅ This is the time to loosen restraints you've placed on your game and move toward something you've wanted to try.

LINE 3 ⋅ Something in your game is extravagant. Your game must know limitations or you will dearly regret it. Once you get this message, hold back something in your game.

LINE 4 ⋅ Do not tire yourself and your game by using too much restraint. Try to live peacefully within the limitations of your game.

LINE 5 ⋅ Play the game within your own limitations. It can be quite pleasurable.

LINE 6 ⋅ You're limiting your game excessively in some way. Don't be severe.

61. CONFIDENCE

sincerity, accordance

The kind of confidence you're looking for has an effect on
every player around you. Each one becomes influenced by it.

This lesson is about confidence and where it comes from. It comes
from the player, of course. Sometimes there is too much, sometimes too
little, sometimes it depends on something outside the player (a coach,
perhaps), sometimes it comes from inside. It is this inner confidence
that a player needs to rely on.

This image is of Arnold Palmer strutting. It symbolizes the qualities of confidence and openheartedness. There was always honesty, truthfulness, and openheartedness about Palmer. It showed in the way he carried himself. It showed in the people who followed him. It was these qualities to which the gallery was attracted. His confidence influenced them.

stages of confidence

LINE 1 ⟩ This is a good time to rely on yourself for your game. Try not to look for outside help. Just depend on yourself.

LINE 2 ⟩ You are developing an inner kind of confidence, a heartfelt desire for your game that awakens others. It may not show, but it is there.

LINE 3 ⟩ Your confidence can be shaken by wide swings of mood. These can come from depending too much on your relationships to partners and others.

LINE 4 ⟩ Locate the source of your confidence, and don't stray from it.

LINE 5 ⟩ Continue to play honestly and confidently and these qualities will begin to link you to other players.

LINE 6 ⟩ Don't be overconfident. You'll just end up crowing with no game to back it up.

62. THE SMALL GET BY

conscientiousness, small gains

*Choose one part of your game to be
conscientious about. A part that has lacked your attention.*

This lesson bears the message not to aim too high (have goals that are too lofty) or be aggressive when playing. This is a time to focus on making your shots small, contained, and not grandiose. It is also suggested that you not be *so* concerned with each and every shot to the degree that you treat them all with reverence.

This image is of Leo Diegel, the player who sensationalized an elbows-out putting technique. This *small, contained style* of putting is symbolic of the fact that the seemingly small part of the game is what makes gains and gets the golfer by. And it is these small, conscientious gains a player needs to attend to at this time.

stages of conscientiousness

LINE 1 ᛣ Attend to getting a sense of when your ball is ready to leave the tee or lie, as if it were a bird leaving the nest for the first time. Too early is not good.

LINE 2 ᛣ Be content with playing modest golf. Even if you've aimed higher.

LINE 3 ᛣ Pay attention to the smallest details of your game. Sometimes these seemingly ineffectual details can hurt your game.

LINE 4 ᛣ In your game, be careful of the temptation to meet some shots with force. Pass them by.

LINE 5 ᛣ You've got sufficient power for your game. It is not readily available. This is the condition you're playing with. Watch players who have learned to play in this condition.

LINE 6 ᛣ Your game will get away from you if you don't attend to each shot. Do not just let your shots fly and play arrogantly.

63. AFTER COMPLETION

accomplishment, fulfillment, achievement, after the end

After you complete your game, it is important to
ritualize it in some way to bring it to a proper close.

This lesson is about what happens between rounds. It is an important transition. What can happen is given over to relaxing completely without reflecting on the parts of your game that have troubled you. This is a time to take a look at some of these shots and muse. The temptation to boil over one's round can also occur. The reflection ought to be done in a cautious and timely manner so as to not lose the importance of the postround ritual.

This image is of Bobby Jones and friends after a round. It is symbolic of completion, a most important part of the game, what a player does afterward, how he behaves toward friends and other players, how he reflects and completes the day.

stages of after completion

LINE 1 · When you've accomplished a successful shot or an entire round, take pause. Practice *not* getting intoxicated with the accomplishment.

LINE 2 · Your game has lost something. Don't go fretting or looking for it because it returns on its own. Keep your equanimity. If it's really yours, it will come back.

LINE 3 · If you've taken on a difficult game, almost attacking it, expect to feel exhausted afterward. It's best not to attack the game so directly next time.

LINE 4 · Even during the greatest round, there will be a shot that sends you reeling. A thoughtful player notes this and doesn't neglect it during the next practice.

LINE 5 · Reflect on where you put too much effort into your game and receive little and where you put in less effort with better timing and more heart and find that the benefits are greater. Appropriate effort never ceases to amaze.

LINE 6 · Sometimes looking back over your game too much can prevent you from completing it and moving forward. Watch for this after completion. Don't take your game apart too much.

64. BEFORE COMPLETION

tasks not yet completed,
before the beginning, before the end

Your game is changing form.
Don't push it. Focus on what you do before you play.

This lesson is not the final lesson because the *Golf Ching* has no end.
This is merely the lesson before lesson one. The crux of this lesson is
about what needs to be done before your game begins. It advises you
not to rush to complete your warm-up, swing, or game. Use this lesson
to curb whatever chaos may be in your game.

This image is of Bobby Jones testing his not yet finished Augusta National, site of the prestigious Masters Tournament, which he designed and built. This image is symbolic of a player's game before beginning, getting ready, just taking form.

stages of before completion

LINE 1 · Treat your game as if it were in the beginning stage. Be cautious. Don't hurry. Don't let unbridled enthusiasm unbalance you.

LINE 2 · Focus on your pregame routine. This is an important part of your game now. It prevents you from moving too quickly.

LINE 3 · Your game as a whole is in a state of transition. You can tend to this by watching carefully how you make the transition from warm-up to the first tee.

LINE 4 · Your game as a whole has gone through a transition. After beginning play, you must leave regrets on the driving range. Make an energetic attempt to build a positive foundation for the game that is to come.

LINE 5 · You're playing a new game. Consider that you've made a transition. Persist in playing the game you know is right for you.

LINE 6 · After your game, have a good time. Don't do anything in excess or you'll lose the trust of your fellow players.

THE CHART

UPPER ➤ LOWER ▼	☰	☱	☲	☳	☴	☵	☶	☷
☰	1	34	5	26	11	9	14	43
☱	25	51	3	27	24	42	21	17
☲	6	40	29	4	7	59	64	47
☳	33	62	39	52	15	53	56	31
☴	12	16	8	23	2	20	35	45
☵	44	32	48	18	46	57	50	28
☶	13	55	63	22	36	37	30	49
☷	10	54	60	41	19	61	38	58

Key for Identifying the Lessons

PHOTO CREDITS

Page no.	Credit
7	St. Andrews University Photographic Collection
8	UPI/Bettmann
10	Culver Pictures
12	United States Golf Association
14	UPI/Corbis-Bettmann
16	UPI/Corbis-Bettmann
18	United States Golf Association
20	UPI/Corbis-Bettmann
22	United States Golf Association
24	Corbis-Bettmann
26	UPI/Corbis-Bettmann
28	Tom Doak
30	UPI/Corbis-Bettmann
32	UPI/Bettmann
34	UPI/Bettmann
36	Corbis-Bettmann
38	UPI/Corbis-Bettmann
40	Underwood & Underwood/Corbis-Bettmann
42	UPI/Bettmann
44	UPI/Corbis-Bettmann
46	Winged Foot Golf Club
48	UPI/Corbis-Bettmann
50	UPI/Bettmann Newsphotos
52	UPI/Bettmann
54	UPI/Corbis-Bettmann

Page no.	Credit
56	UPI/Corbis-Bettmann
58	Underwood & Underwood/Corbis-Bettmann
60	St. Andrews University Photographic Collection
62	UPI/Bettmann Newsphotos
64	UPI/Bettmann
66	Hy Peskin/Life Magazine © Time Warner Inc.
68	UPI/Corbis-Bettmann
70	St. Andrews University Photographic Collection
72	UPI/Corbis-Bettmann
74	The Bettmann Archive
76	Corbis-Bettmann
76	UPI/Bettmann
78	UPI/Corbis-Bettmann
80	United States Golf Association
82	UPI/Bettmann
84	UPI/Bettmann
86	UPI/Corbis-Bettmann
88	UPI/Corbis-Bettmann
90	UPI/Bettmann
92	Underwood & Underwood/Corbis-Bettmann
94	Underwood & Underwood/Corbis-Bettmann
96	UPI/Bettmann
98	UPI/Bettmann
100	UPI/Corbis-Bettmann
102	UPI/Bettmann
104	UPI/Corbis-Bettmann
106	UPI/Bettmann
108	UPI/Bettmann
110	UPI/Bettmann
112	UPI/Bettmann
114	UPI/Corbis-Bettmann
116	Corbis-Bettmann
118	Underwood & Underwood/Corbis-Bettmann
120	UPI/Bettmann
122	UPI/Bettmann

Page no.	Credit
124	UPI/Corbis-Bettmann
126	Corbis-Bettmann
128	UPI/Bettmann
130	UPI/Bettmann Newsphotos
132	United States Golf Association
134	UPI/Bettmann